PLACE NAMES OF THE CAMDEN AREA

Brian Burnett, Janice Johnson,
Richard Nixon, John Wrigley

Camden Historical Society

Published by Camden Historical Society Inc.

40 John Street, Camden, NSW 2570
(SAN: 908 3002)

www.camdenhistory.com.au

The Estate of the late Janice Johnson, who died in 2017, provided the funds to publish this book.

© 2022 by the Camden Historical Society Inc.

All rights reserved. No part of this publication may be used or reproduced without written permission, except for brief quotations in critical articles and reviews. Contact the Camden Historical Society PO Box 566 Camden NSW 2570 Australia for more information. (secretary@camdenhistory.org.au)

First published in 2005
Second Edition 2022

2nd Edition

ISBN: 978-0-6485894-1-9

Front cover: Macaria, Camden – Ian Willis

Front & back cover: The aerial photo was taken from a balloon in 1994: Photographer – Rosemary Gibson.

Contents

Contents	iii
Introduction	1
Alphabetical Place Names	3
Parish Map Locations	73
The Township of Camden 1850s	97
Camden Park Estate Sales	99
Bibliography	110
Index to Landowners, Tenants, and Others	111

Introduction

Camden and its adjoining regions are rapidly changing. There are housing developments and shopping centres where there were green pastures and cattle only a decade ago. Sydney's urban sprawl is now on our doorstep. Our rural landscape has been irrevocably changed. New names have been given to well-known places and landmarks.

The first edition of this book drew together the knowledge of many members of the Camden Historical Society, the Camden Area Family History Society and information from the archives of both organisations. This revised edition includes the previous information, in some instances amended, and maps held by Camden Historical Society that show where the grants were given and properties established.

In scrutinising the maps, additional properties have been identified and their history checked. Land grants have also been verified. Many of the place names listed are obscure or were the names of properties or houses that no longer exist. Some names are no longer in general use, and some are now known to only a few people. From personal experience, we understand that a name or one word can be remembered from childhood, or a locality may be mentioned on birth, marriage, or death certificates. The dates shown after a person's name are their dates of birth and death, if known.

Originals of the maps included in this book may be inspected at the map cabinet of the Camden Museum Archives and include both Parish Maps and Land Sale Maps. Each provides a wealth of information. Readers are also encouraged to use the Google search engine, where it is possible to locate street addresses and photos of a property.

By recording the place names in this book, it is hoped that the names and their meanings will be preserved for future researchers. An index of landowners, tenants, and others has also been provided in this edition to further aid researchers.

The assistance of residents in providing information on properties and their tenants is gratefully acknowledged. Without the knowledge provided by John Burge, Len English, Annette Macarthur-Onslow, Richard Nixon and Joy Thorn, some places might have been forgotten, or their heritage lost

This second edition has been dramatically improved by research undertaken by the late Janice Johnson. She made a provision in her will to pay for publishing this edition. Other Camden Historical Society members contributing to this edition include Robert Lester, Robert Wheeler, and Julie Wrigley. The Society thanks Fletcher Joss and Egarag Pty Ltd for editing Janice's publication.

Readers who wish to suggest corrections or additions should put them in writing and contact the Secretary of the Camden Historical Society, 40 John Street, Camden, 2570 or by email at secretary@camdenhistory.org.au

Camden Historical Society 2022

Alphabetical Place Names

ABBOTSFORD   Map 5–1; 6–1

A grant of 400 acres in 1822 (Portion 136, Parish of Picton) to George Harper (1799-1841), north of Picton. He also received a grant of 4200 acres in 1822 near The Oaks. The land extended from the Stonequarry Bridge along Barkers Lodge Road to The Oaks. Harper, a public servant, natural history collector and settler, named his grant Abbotsford as a tribute to his benefactor Sir Walter Scott (1771-1832). Scott died at his home in Abbotsford, Roxburghshire, Scotland. Harper built the George IV Inn at Picton in 1839. (See George IV Inn)

ALLAMBIE

The house at 48 Menangle Road, Camden, was the residence of Guy Francis Wright (1885-1946) and his family. Wright was the manager of Camden Park Estate.

ALPHA COTTAGE

Alpha Cottage no longer exists but was located on the southern corner of John and Mitchell Streets, Camden. Dr Josiah Wesley Walker (1810-1879), one of Camden's early medical practitioners, built the house about 1850. Later, it was owned by John Benson Martin (1818-1908), Camden's long-time Clerk of the Court. The house was demolished in c.1958 for the erection of a new Catholic Presbytery.

AMAROO

Amaroo was the property of William Daniel Cleary at 133 Macquarie Grove Road, Cobbitty, adjacent to Camden Airport.

ANDERSON MEMORIAL FOUNTAIN

The fountain once stood at the corner of Argyle and John Streets (where the current roundabout is located). It was a gift from Frances Lillian Anderson, née Faithfull (1857-1948) and her daughter Clarice Vivian Faithfull-Anderson (1900-1979) in memory of William Hugh Anderson (1869-1912). After several incidents with the night soil cart, the fountain was removed to Macarthur Park. (See Macarthur Park)

ANSCHAU FARM   Map 1–1

Johann (John) Anschau (1834-1908) and his family arrived from Germany to work as vinedressers. Anschau and his brothers purchased four blocks of land in the Weromba area: fifty-eight acres (Portion 106, Parish of Weromba), 58 acres (Portion 126, Parish of Weromba), 66 acres (Portion 102, Parish of Weromba), and seventy-six acres (Portion 103, Parish of Weromba). There they planted their vineyards. Werombi is the modern spelling of Weromba.

APPERL   Map 5–2; 6–2

A grant of 600 acres (Portion 14, Parish of Picton) to Rev William Cowper (1778-1858) adjacent to Fairy Hill.

APPLE TREE FLAT

Apple Tree Flat is between Cawdor Road and Hume Highway, west of Camden Valley Inn. It was the main lucerne growing area on Camden Park Estate.

Alphabetical Place Names

APPLEWOOD

The property of Richard Reginald Inglis (1920-2014) and Lorna Mary née McIntosh at 415 Cobbitty Road, Cobbitty. Previously part of the Denbigh property.

ARCHIES CROSSING

The crossing is a ford of the Nepean River on the road between Menangle and Appin. It was named after Archibald (Archie) Tulloh (1870-1938), a delivery man carrying groceries, meat etc., to Appin from the Menangle General Store twice weekly. Originally known as Bird's Eye Crossing. (See Birds Eye Crossing)

ARENDAL

Arendal is a log-cabin-style weatherboard house at 111 Cobbitty Road, Cobbitty, built by Lars Halvorsen of the well-known boating family Lars Halvorsen Sons Pty Ltd of Sydney as a country weekender. It was named for his birthplace Arendal in the south of Norway. Later owners were Teen Ranch, William Macaulay and Brian Charles Baigent (1929-2000).

ARNOLD'S PUBLIC HOUSE

The original name for the Plough and Harrow Inn. (See Plough and Harrow Inn)

ASTON

A dairy property located on the Brownlow Hill holding at 615 Werombi Road, Brownlow Hill. Former home of Rupert Frederick Arding Downes (1886-1954) and Katie May Elizabeth Coghill Downes, née Maddrell.

AUSTRALIAN NURSERY

(See Ferguson's Nursery)

AVENEL

The brick house at 44 Menangle Road, Camden, was built by John Peat (1864-1955) for Charles Ernest Doust (1884-1947) and Emma Catherine née Burrell (1889-1970) and later owned by Noel Frederick Boardman and Christine Loris née McLean.

BADGALLY   Map 10–1

Formerly the property of Edward Lomas Moore (1822-1887). Now St Gregory's Marist Brothers College.

Currently, Badgally is a location and the name of a road on the northwestern side of Campbelltown.

An alternate spelling is Badgelly.

BALLYMACAMMON   Map 8–1; 12–1

A grant of 470 acres in 1815 (Portion 13, Parish of Cook) to John Thomas Campbell (1770-1830) near Greendale.

BALMORAL COTTAGE

The property of Malcom McNiven (1810-1858) and Sarah née McLean (1814-1893). The McNiven's were early settlers at Mount Hunter.

BALWEARIE

The residence was built for Arthur John (Jack) Macarthur-Onslow (1873-1953) and Christian Leslie, née Bell, Camden, in the early 1900s. Designed by Sulman and named after a home in Scotland. Later renamed Murrandah by subsequent occupants Lt. Col. (later Brigadier General) George MacLeay Macarthur-Onslow (1875-1931) and Violet Marguerite Macarthur-Onslow née Gordon (1879-1981). Now the Camden Nursing Home, Old Hume Highway, South Camden. (See Murrandah)

BANGOR

Bangor was the home of Ronald Andrew McIntosh and Mary Stratford, née Sharpe, on a part of the old Denbigh property at Cobbitty.

BANK OF NSW   Map 20

The first bank in Camden was the Bank of NSW which opened in 1865 at 29 Argyle Street. In 2019 the building was the office of funeral directors White Ladies. In 1868 the bank transferred to new premises, the former Woolpack Hotel. (See Woolpack Hotel)

BARRAGAL LAGOON

Barragal Lagoon is near Menangle on Camden Park. Governor Lachlan Macquarie is reputed to have camped there on 16 November 1810.

BARSHAM

A property purchased by Peter Miller (1839-1922) at Hoxton Park was named for his birthplace, East Barsham, Norfolk, England. Miller's name was given to the suburb of Miller.

BATHURST FARM   Map 12–2

A grant of 1500 acres in 1816 (Portion 7, Parish of Cook) to Captain John Piper (1773-1851), military officer and public servant.

BELGENNY

An Aboriginal word meaning 'dry land.' (Alternative spellings are Benkennie and Benhennie.) The Aboriginal name for the area of South Camden near Belgenny Farm.

BELGENNY FARM or HOME FARM

Located at 100 Elizabeth Macarthur Avenue, Camden, this historic collection of buildings was the working farm centre of the Camden Park Estate. Previously known as The Farm and later as The Home Farm. Currently operated by The Belgenny Trust and open to the public and schools.

BELGENNY LAGOON

Belgenny Lagoon is on Camden Park, just northeast of the Camden Park mansion and buildings. (See Spectacle Pond)

BELLFIELD FARM

A grant of four hundred acres in 1818 (Portion 30, Parish of Cabramatta) to Edward Gray (1791-1868). A later owner was Robin (Robert) Bell (1785-1861), who moved to the Hunter district.

BELMONT   Map 17–1; 18–1

An early grant of 2000 acres in 1805 (Portion 2, Parish of Camden), on the western side of the Nepean River at Menangle, to Walter Stevenson Davidson (1785-1869). Davidson was a merchant banker friend of the Macarthur family and sold the property to James and William Macarthur as an addition to Camden Park. (See Camden Park)

BELVEDERE - CAMDEN

The house at 59 Menangle Road, Camden, was built in 1906 for Philip Benjamin (Ben) Hodge (1877-1979) and Maud née Huthnance. Restored and extended in 2003.

BELVEDERE - Elderslie

The house was originally located at 40 River Road, Elderslie, the home of Francesco Giuseppe Carmagnola (1900-1986) and his family. It was relocated to a Menangle Road frontage but fell into disrepair and has since been demolished.

BENKENNIE

Benkennie is the alternative spelling of the Aboriginal name Belgenny.

BEN LINDEN

Ben Linden is the private home at 311 Camden Valley Way, Narellan. The home was operated as a maternity hospital by Nurse E Jean Stuckey in the early and mid-twentieth century.

BENTS BASIN   Map 8–2; 16–1

Bents Basin is on the Nepean River near Greendale, west of Shankamore. Originally part of the grant Mousley to Ellis Bent (1783-1815). Now a State Recreation Area. (See Mousley)

BENWERRIN

Benwerrin is at 120 The Old Oaks Road, Grasmere. Previous owners were Gladys Ivy Hedley, the wife of James Hedley and John Carlyle Southwell and his family.

BERGINS WEIR   Map 7–1

Bergins Weir was on the Nepean River near Menangle Park, downstream of Menangle Bridge between the Menangle Weir and Thurn's Weir. The weir is named after Edward Bergin (1842-1924), who owned Tinehurst Glenlee — also known as Glenlee Weir. According to WaterNSW, the weir has collapsed. (See Weirs)

BERNERA

The homestead on the estate was built by Allan Macpherson (1818-1891) in 1857 at Hoxton Park. Macpherson was a son of a former Collector of Internal Revenue, William Macpherson (1784-1866). The estate was a vineyard and grew hay and maize. Bernera was listed on the Register of the National Estate until 1986, when it was destroyed by fire. In 1889 the estate was subdivided into ninety-four farming allotments of about ten acres each. Liverpool historians Ward and Olive Havard occupied the original homestead for decades until 1985.

BETHSHEEN

A heritage-listed home was built for James Funnell (1830-1918) at 285 Cobbitty Road, Cobbitty, between Stoneleigh and Wyembah. Funnell was a wheelwright. It was sold to Mary Ann Rebecca New née Funnell (1864-1935) in 1912 and owned by George Henry Wales (1890-1992) and his family from 1929 to 1972. They gave it the name Bethsheen, sometimes referred to as Blacksmiths Cottage.

BICKLEY VALE – Camden

A house owned by William Sidman (1847-1917) and family at 69 John Street, Camden. The house was demolished in 1984 for the erection of the Camden Senior Citizens' Centre.

BICKLEY VALE – Mount Hunter

The area between Cawdor Road and Mount Hunter was a property owned by Howard Carlyle Southwell (1899-1951) and his family.

BIG HILL

A hill located on Big Hill Road, connecting Glenmore to Silverdale Road.

BIG SANDY

Big Sandy is a deep-water swimming area on the Nepean River in King's Bush. It is about 100 metres downstream from Little Sandy Bridge. The Camden Swimming Club built the first dressing sheds in Camden at the site. (See King's Bush)

BIRDS EYE CROSSING

A crossing place on the Nepean River at Menangle. Later known as Archie's Crossing. (See Archies Crossing)

BIRLING   Map 9–1; 13–1

A grant of 1000 acres on 28 August 1812 (Portion 50, Parish of Cook) to Robert Lowe (1783-1832). Bushranger Jack Donohue was taken to Birling after being shot in 1830, located north of Maryland in Bringelly. The house is heritage-listed.

BLACKSMITHS COTTAGE

A heritage-listed home at 285 Cobbitty Road, Cobbitty is better known as Bethsheen. (See Bethsheen)

BLAIR ATHOL HOUSE

A prominent two-storey home on Blair Athol Drive Campbelltown. The residence of John Kidd (1838-1919), storekeeper, dairy farmer, and Member of Parliament for Camden. It was named after a small town in Scotland. Now a housing estate named Blair Athol.

BLARNEY

Blarney is the grassed slope on the eastern side of Camden Park Garden, where flowering bulbs are traditionally grown.

BOBS RANGE

Bobs Range is an area south of Werombi Road, west of Brownlow Hill and north of The Oaks.

BOULTON FARM

The farm was initially leased by former convict John Boulton (1794-1881) from Camden Park. In 1884 it was owned by George William Cooper (1856-1907).

BOSWORTH FARM   Map 15–1

A grant of 200 acres in 1816 (Portion 9, Parish of Cook) to Samuel Otto Hassall (1796-1830) on Cut Hill Road, Cobbitty. The old house was the residence of the Fryer family for nearly fifty years until it burned down in the early 1900s. A new house was built by Fieldhouse for John Thomas McMinn (1834-1913) and his family but was demolished in 2004. For a time, it was owned by the Teen Ranch organisation.

BOYS HOME

A two-storey late nineteenth-century home at 56a Ferguson Road, West Camden, operated as a residential home for boys until the 1940s. At one time known as The Society, Special Mission to Waifs and Strays. Now a private residence. (See Macquarie House)

BRACKFIELD FARM

A grant of fifty acres in 1818 to John Brackfield (1773-1824) at South Creek. Brackfield arrived in the Colony in 1799 as a convict. His farm was successful. On 13 November 1824, he was murdered in his home by a gang of thieves. Later the property was owned by Richard Smythe, who in 1848 sold the property to James John Curry (1826-1916).

BRANSBYS COTTAGE

The cottage is a building at 17 Mitchell Street Camden and may be the oldest surviving building in Camden. The site was auctioned in 1841. The colonial-style Georgian cottage was built between 1842-1843. Charles Kemp purchased the property in 1846 from Thomas Cox. Kemp leased the house, and one of its earliest tenants was Dr George Bransby (1810-1897). Bransby was a medical practitioner, coroner and magistrate who moved to Camden in January 1848. In 1852 Kemp sold the property to John Lakeman. Also known as Taplin's Cottage after William Leslie Taplin (1891-1977). In the 1990s, the cottage was extensively restored by the owners.

BRICKYARDS

Several brickyards were in the area

- The corner of Macquarie Grove Road and Exeter Street in 1840 was known as No. 1 Kiln. The bricks for Harrington Park are sourced from this kiln together with the first layers of bricks for St John's Church. It was the first known brickyard in the district.
- Argyle Street near Cowpasture Bridge 1840-1850, later site of Tweed Mill. The mill was known as No. 2 Kiln. Bricks for St John's Church and the first Steam Mill came from this location.
- Edward Street 1880-1940s. This yard made the bricks for Studley Park House, Camelot, and Carrington Hospital.
- South Argyle Street 1850s-1900.
- Somerset Avenue Narellan 1870s-1900s.
- Corner Cawdor Road, Murray, and Barsden Streets WWI to 1944.
- Queen Street Narellan.

BRINGELLY Map 8–3; 9–2

A grant of 220 acres on 13 January 1818 (Portion 20, Parish of Cabramatta) to William Hutchinson (1772-1846). Named for Robert Lowe's wife, Barbara née Willard (1783-1818), birthplace in Sussex, England. The origin of the suburb name.

BRISBANE FARM Map 4–1; 17–2; 18–2; 19-1

A grant of 4368 acres in 1823 (Portion 10, Parish of Camden) to John Macarthur. (See Camden Park)

BRISBANE MEADOWS

It was part of Brisbane Farm at Mount Hunter, the location of Whites Farm (after Robert White 1862-1919) and Bourke's Dam (after Thomas Bourke 1822-1881). It was a watering hole for teamsters on the south side of Moore's Way.

BROOKS FLAT

Brooks Flat was the first individual farm established on the property of Thomas Dawson (1820-1893) at Mount Hunter.

BROOKFIELD HOUSE

This sizeable two-storey terrace house is at 30-32 Hill Street Camden. The Macarthur-Onslow family built the house to provide accommodation for officers of the NSW Mounted Rifles. It was previously the site of the Old Roman Catholic Presbytery. One early resident was Major Henry Beauchamp Lassetter (1860-1926).

BROOKSIDE

Near Jarvisfield Picton. Racecourse Creek runs through the property.

BROWFIELD

A portion of the Hardwick estate on Wattle Creek was purchased by Edward Whybrow (1815-1896) with the financial assistance of Henry Thompson (1820-1871). After Whybrow's death, the property was held by his son, William Edward Whybrow (1857-1916), until the early 1900s. The property's name combines the surnames of Whybrow and his wife, Julia Whybrow, née Field's maiden name.

BROWNLOW HILL Map 2–1; 8–4

A grant of 1663 acres in 1825 (Portion 93, Parish of Weromba) to Alexander MacLeay (1767-1848), then Colonial Secretary of the Colony. A further 2000 acres to the south, originally granted to Peter Murdoch (1795-1871), and named Glendaruel, was later added. Captain Charles Sturt commenced his Darling River expedition from Brownlow Hill. The property was later owned by George MacLeay (1809-1891).

BROWNLOW HILL WEIR

Brownlow Hill Weir is on the Nepean River downstream of the Mount Hunter Rivulet Weir and Cobbitty Bridge and upstream of Campbell's Ford at Greendale. There is an association with Frederick William Arthur Downes (1855-1917). The structure is a concrete fixed crest weir approximately 1.8 metres high and 51.2 metres across, completed by 1912. The weir is heritage-listed and still in good condition. (See Weirs)

BRUCHHAUSER HOUSE

Located at 23 Bruchhauser Crescent Elderslie built by Johann Bruchhauser (1820-1901). Bruchhauser had arrived as a vinedresser to work on Camden Park. He later purchased land at Elderslie and became a successful orchard.

BRUSH

Phillip Cox designed this house in Camden Park for Dame Helen Blaxland in the 1980s. It was in the early vineyard area of the Macarthurs at Camden Park.

BUCKINGHAM   Map 10–3

A grant of 400 acres in 1810 (Portion 45, Parish of Narellan) to Gabriel Louis Marie Huon de Kerilleau (1769-1828). De Kerilleau was from Brittany in France. Before 1810 he had been a tutor to John Macarthur's sons at Parramatta. The small rough brick home built by de Kerilleau became the police lock-up after a larger house was built by James Chisholm Jr. (1806-1888). It later became part of Gledswood. (See Gledswood)

BUGGY'S FARM

A grant of one hundred acres (Portion 61, Parish of Weromba) and the adjoining Portion 80, Parish of Weromba, was purchased by Michael Buggy (1798-1881) and Anne Buggy, née Kenna.

BUGGY'S HILL

Buggy's Hill is a disused name for the rising hill from Theresa Park to Bobs Range. The hill is named for Michael Buggy (1798-1881), who owned the property containing the hill.

BULLBED

Bullbed is the name of the lower southeastern slopes of Razorback between Douglas Park and Maldon. The location was named by Ensign Francis Louis Barrallier (1773-1853) in 1802 because he saw the fighting ground of the bulls from the wild cattle herd.

BULLECOURT

A weatherboard cottage at 49 Broughton Street, Camden, built about 1920 by members of the Volunteer Workers Association for the injured returned WWI serviceman Bartley Horace Chesham (1895-1950). Bullecourt was restored in 2002. It was named for the WWI Battle of Bullecourt in which he participated.

BURNHAM GROVE ESTATE

The property at 332 Cawdor Road, Cawdor, was owned by Frederick Joseph Doust (1864-1900) and his family and later Raymond Charles Wheeler (1897-1964) and Bertha Florist Wheeler née Doust (1899-1973). Burnham Grove is said to be a copy of the original Mount Hercules Homestead. Now a historic home and wedding venue.

BURTON ARMS HOTEL

The hotel was located at 332 Camden Valley Way, Narellan. It was built in the 1830s. Later became a store owned by Ephraim Cross Jr. (1867-1942), then Bob Stevens' Auto Electrics. Currently a Real Estate office.

BUTTER FACTORY

Several butter factories or creameries were located around the district

- Camden – The Camden Refrigerating, Butter Making and Bacon Curing Works opened in 1896 in Elizabeth Street on the corner of Station Street, with the whole frontage paralleling the main line of the railway at the Camden Station terminus. The factory closed in 1899, and it was later demolished.
- Cobbitty – 167 Cobbitty Road, Cobbitty. Now a home that is known as Riverview.
- Menangle – known as the Menangle Central Creamery, which ran from the 1880s, Located southern portion of Lot 21 of DP 581462, a parcel of land to the west of Menangle Railway Station, with road access from Stevens Road, off Station Street. Closed and building currently not used.
- Mount Hunter - was located near the Mount Hunter Rivulet on Burragorang Road, now demolished.

(See Creameries)

CABRAMATTA   Map 9–3; 10–4; 11–1

This name is thought to be from Aboriginal words meaning fresh, tasty water grub and a point or jutting out piece of land. Site of a grant of 700 acres in 1808 to Sir John Jamison (1786-1844), which he named Cow-de-Knaves. The name Cow-de-Knaves today refers to trig station TS10703 at Austral. Cabramatta was originally the name for Rossmore. (See Cow-de-Knaves)

CADBROUGH HILL

Part of the Razorback Range.

CAERNARVON

It was located at 180 Macquarie Grove Road, Kirkham, north of Nepean River and owned by Thomas Sheil (1828-1907).

CALDER FARM

A grant of 170 acres on 13 January 1818 (Portion 41, Parish of Narellan) to James Chisholm (1772-1837). Located east of Molles Main, Narellan, it is bounded northeast by Connor's Farm, northwest by Mitchell's Farm and southwest by Molles Main. Chisholm named the farm after his birthplace, Calder, Edinburgh, Scotland. It later became part of Gledswood. (See Gledswood)

CALF FARM - Menangle

It is located on the Camden Park Estate at Menangle. Also, the name of a location on a former calf-rearing farm at Mount Hunter at the end of Spring Creek Road.

CALMSLEY

The home and property of the family of Frank Dengate (1850-1929) in Hilder Street Elderslie.

CAMBERFIELD

A plateau at the top of old Razorback running westward. Farmed by Edward Tickner (1789-1864), then his son-in-law Frederick James Dengate (1839-1901), and then Richard Ernest Hawkey (1873-1952). Part of this land was initially reserved as Church and School land.

Alphabetical Place Names

CAMDEN Map 17–3; 18–3; 20

John Macarthur returned to Sydney in 1805 with orders for a grant of part of the best pastureland in the Colony from Lord Camden, British Secretary of State of the Colonies. Macarthur named his grant Camden. The Macarthur family changed the estate's name to Camden Park to avoid confusion with the new village of Camden. James and William Macarthur established the town after John Macarthur's death, with plans drawn up in 1836, and the first land sale was in 1840. In the 1850s, an alternate name for the town was Camden Village.

The town's main street layout still reflects the original plan by Thomas Mitchell.

CAMDEN ACRES

A property on Camden Valley Way west of Studley Park with a house built after 1934 by Leo Daniel Whyte (1887-1975) and Florence June née Baker and subdivided in 2005 for a housing estate.

CAMDEN COMMON

Camden Common was an area of land for public use in early Camden. Located on the southern side of the junction of Cawdor Road and Barsden Street, also called The Common. Teamsters often camped on this land.

CAMDEN COTTAGE

39 John Street Camden was built in the 1840s, next to the Macaria. Purchased by Henry Thompson (1820-1871) on April 20, 1855, when he bought a half-acre allotment in John Street from the estate of Sarah Middlehurst, née Milford (previously Tiffin) (1807-1854). Sarah was the housekeeper at Camden Park. She had purchased the property from the Macarthurs with money inherited from her father, John Milford. She then erected a building she rented from 1844 at £20 p.a. to the Camden Bench for use as the Police Station, police Constable's Residence and Court House.

It is also known as "Sarah Tiffen's Cottage" and was the home of Charles Augustus Thompson (1847-1929). Later the home of Willie Larkin (1870-1963) and known as Larkins Cottage. In 2019 the property was a gift shop and café.

CAMDEN COURT HOUSE Map 20

Camden Court House at 31 John Street Camden is built on land set aside for this purpose by James and William Macarthur at the time the town allotment plans were laid down. The brothers also offered £100 towards the cost of building.

The first buildings on this site were a timber lock-up and a Chief Constable's residence. The present building was commenced in 1855 and completed in 1857 with cells underneath and at the rear. The building was designed during William Weaver's term as Government Architect. A new lock-up was built from 1859-1861 to replace the old one.

CAMDEN FARM

The name was used in the 1840–1850s for Belgenny. (See Belgenny and Camden Park)

CAMDEN FIRE STATION

The former fire station at 40 John Street Camden was built in 1867 as the Temperance Hall. The hall was used for Camden Council Meetings until 1889, when Council meetings moved to the

Camden School of Arts. The facade was added when the Temperance Hall was transformed into the Camden Fire Station. The building now forms part of the Camden Library complex.

CAMDEN GENERAL CEMETERY   Map 7–2

Located at 201 Cawdor Road on the eastern side and north of Burragorang Road, it was consecrated on 23 June 1898. It is still Camden's main operating cemetery, recently enhanced by Camden Council.

CAMDEN HOTEL

Formerly the Commercial Hotel. (See Commercial Hotel)

CAMDEN INN

The Macarthurs built the Camden Inn on the corner of Argyle and Elizabeth Streets. The first licensee in 1842 was Joseph Thomas Goodluck (1806-1845) (sometimes Goodlucke). The second licensee was John Lakeman (1811-1869), who subsequently purchased the property. John Galvin (1821-1865) purchased the inn in 1855 from Lakeman. Later publicans include Thomas Carroll and, in 1896, Annie French, previously of the Commercial Hotel. From 1900 it was known as the Royal Hotel and later the Merino Tavern. The present owners have reverted to the name Royal Hotel. (See Royal Hotel)

CAMDEN MASONIC TEMPLE HALL

The hall is located at 36 Hill Street and was built by Percival Ernest Butler (1880-1929) in 1926 on what was formerly the St John's Parochial School site. (See St John's Parochial School)

CAMDEN MUSEUM

The Camden Museum is a local history museum at 40 John Street, operated by Camden Historical Society Inc. since 1970. The museum is located on the site of the former Camden School of Arts, now part of the Camden Library /Museum complex.

CAMDEN PARK   Map 17–4; 18–4

It started with a grant in 1805 (Portion 1, Parish of Camden) to John Macarthur (1786-1834) and was initially called Camden. The grants which made up Camden Park were Camden Park (2250 acres), Upper Camden (2750 acres), Belmont (2000 acres), South Camden (1565 acres), West Camden (2065 acres), Brisbane Farm (4368 acres), Cawdor (5000 acres), North Camden (5400 acres), Rosslyn (1150 acres), and Melrose (1150 acres), a total of 27,698 acres. Camden was named after Lord Camden, British Secretary of State for the Colonies, in 1804. From 1829 it was known as Camden Park, which suggested appreciating open vistas as part of a close relationship with nature. (See Camden Park House). About 1000 acres are still operated by the Macarthur family, mainly as a dairy.

CAMDEN PARK CREAMERY

Now part of Belgenny, it started as a carriage house on Camden Park in the 1820s. It was later converted into a creamery. The creamery later moved to Menangle Central Creamery. (See Menangle Central Creamery and Butter Factory)

CAMDEN PARK GATE LODGE – Camden

The house at 224 Old Hume Highway Camden was designed for Elizabeth Macarthur-Onslow by Sir John Sulman and is of Federation period construction, with weatherboard walls, brick chimneys, decorative half-timbered gables, and a terracotta tiled roof. The east and north-facing gables carried the coats-of-arms of the Macarthur and Onslow families; one of the plaques has since been removed.

CAMDEN PARK GATE LODGE – Menangle

A house on Woodbridge Road, Menangle, was designed for Elizabeth Macarthur-Onslow by Sir John Sulman and is of Federation period construction, with weatherboard walls, brick chimneys, decorative half-timbered gables, and a terracotta tiled roof. The east-facing and north-facing gables carry the coats-of-arms of the Macarthur and Onslow families. It is now part of the Elizabeth Macarthur Agricultural Institute.

CAMDEN PARK HOUSE

Work began on the house in 1831 to a design by the architect John Verge and was finished about 1835. Verge's design for the house was based on the Palladian principle of a central two-storied block flanked by symmetrical pavilions; the pavilion to the northwest extended into an enclosed courtyard. The house was built of stuccoed sandstock brick on sandstone foundations, which doubled as a cellar. Window mouldings, porticos, parapets and the single-piece columns were made of the local Hawkesbury sandstone. The labour was provided by convicts assigned to the Macarthurs.

Although based on a European pattern, Verge's house design has proved appropriate for the extremes of the Australian climate and the changing patterns of social behaviour. The only major addition occurred in the 1880s when a second storey was added to the northwest wing. The informal layout of the rooms contrasts with the formal exterior and accurately reflects the fashions of the 1830s.

CAMDEN PICTURE THEATRE – THE PARAMOUNT

The building at 39 Elizabeth Street, Camden, was Camden's second picture theatre. It was built during the depression years and was first operated by Philip John (Jack) Fox (1890-1958) and James Frederick John Pinkerton (1878-1936). The picture theatre opened in 1933 and closed in 1961. In 2019 it was a tyre service outlet.

CAMDEN POLICE STATION — Map 20

Camden Police Station at 35 John Street, Camden, was built in 1878. Earlier, the police presence was maintained with a timber lock-up and adjoining residence for the Chief Constable on the present courthouse site.

The barracks are a good example of the police buildings for that period. The verandah was once enclosed but has been fully restored in recent times. However, it is no longer used as a Police Station since the new Local Area Command Police Station was opened at Narellan on Friday, 12 August 2011.

CAMDEN POST OFFICE — Map 20

The first post office in Camden was in the front section of a cottage in Argyle Street next door to the Camden Inn on the corner of Argyle and Elizabeth Streets. It operated from 1 May 1841, with the first postmistress being Eliza Pearson (1803-1879). By 1848 Camden was part of a daily mail coach service from Sydney to Goulburn.

A Telegraph Office was opened in 1877 in Argyle Street next door to the Plough and Harrow, and in 1878 it was proposed to combine the two offices into a government-built building. Tenders were called, and a post office on the present site, 135 Argyle Street, was completed on 8 February

1882. At that time, it consisted of a 20-foot by 15-foot office, four rooms, a servant's room, and a kitchen. Additional improvements, including a second storey for the residence and a balcony above the public area, were approved in 1897. It still operates as Camden's Post Office and has a National Heritage listing.

CAMDEN RAILWAY STATION   Map 20 and 25

Until 1901 the Camden Railway Station was located on the northern side of Argyle Street on the corner of Edward Street, with the terminus on the southern side of Argyle Street on the corner of View Street. The Camden Refrigeration, Butter Making and Bacon Curing Works were in Elizabeth Street with a spur line and platform in Edward Street to facilitate loading their products. The station in Argyle Street is marked on a land sale map dated 13 and 14 March 1898. However, a map prepared for the North Cawdor Estate sales in 1887 also indicates a train platform in Edward Street.

In May 1901, a decision was made to move the Camden Station and terminus to Edward Street. The Camden line to Campbelltown operated until late 1962, when it formally closed. The last train ran on New Year's Day, 1963, with a special train bringing many people for their last ride. A DVD about the line is available at Camden Museum. The station area is currently the site of a machinery sales yard and a food outlet.

CAMDEN REFRIGERATION, BUTTER MAKING AND BACON CURING WORKS

This business opened in Elizabeth Street on the corner of Station Street, Camden, in April 1886. The factory ceased operating in 1898 after sustaining severe damage in the flood of February 1898, and the processing was moved to Menangle. (See Camden Railway Station)

CAMDEN SCHOOL OF ARTS

This building at 40 John Street, Camden, originally opened in 1866 and provided a Library in the front of a two-storey section and a hall at the rear. The Camden Municipal Council (as it was then known) held its first meeting in the hall in 1889. The Council later took complete control of the building and, in 1963, demolished the two-storey front section and erected a single-storey structure to replace it. The building in 2019 is the Camden Library, and the old hall is the Adult Fiction section. Original windows from the old hall are still in place.

CAMDEN STEAM MILL

The first steam mill commenced in 1840, with Henry Thompson (1820-1871) being the miller. The first mill was in Argyle Street, a little further back but near where the former Milk Depot can be seen. Henry's brother, Samuel Herbert Thompson (1821-1910), ran the adjoining general store on Edward Street. Samuel left the district in 1850, and the store was run by Henry's wife, Anne née Bardwell. The mill's success saw Henry build larger premises on the opposite side of Argyle Street in 1860. The old steam mill was demolished in the 1870s, and the bricks were used to extend the chancel of St John's Church. (See Thompson's Steam Mill and Camden Woollen Mills)

CAMDEN STOCKYARDS

The Stock Yards in Edward Street were initially situated behind the Plough and Harrow Inn in today's Larkin Place. The weekly stock market began in 1867 under William Inglis (1832-1896). In 1940 the Stock Yards moved to their current location.

Alphabetical Place Names

CAMDEN TOWN FARM   Map 25

Camden Town Farm borders Exeter Street and Macquarie Grove Road. Lots 5, 6 and 7 were originally leased from the Camden Park Estate by H. Head. At the time of the North Cawdor Estate sales, the land was purchased by Evan Alfred Davies (1865-1954). His daughter Llewella Hope Evan Davies OAM (1901-2000) bequeathed the property to the people of Camden. A community garden is located here.

CAMDEN VALE MILK DEPOT

Located on the corner of Edward and Argyle Streets, Camden, the building has a commemorative stone dated 8 September 1926. The original timber building burned down in 1926, and the current building was opened in 1927. The building ceased to operate as a Milk Depot in the 1960s. Once the home of Camden Bike & Power. In 2022 it was empty, awaiting re-development.

CAMDEN VALLEY INN

Formerly called the Camden Vale Inn. An English-style inn on the Hume Highway (now 290 Remembrance Drive), South Camden. It was built in 1939 as a milk bar by the Macarthur-Onslow family and the Camden Park Estate. Edward Arthur Macarthur-Onslow (1909-1980) and Winifred Hall, née Owen, initiated the project and the charming design of the building. The architect was Cyril Ruard, and the builder was Herbert Thomas English (1885-1958). In 2019 it was extensively renovated.

CAMDEN VALLEY WAY

Camden Valley Way is a recent name for the Hume Highway from Leppington to Camden.

CAMDEN VINEYARD

Term for the vineyard at Camden Park used from the 1850s onwards. Award-winning wines were produced.

CAMDEN WEIR   Map 7-3

Camden Weir is on Nepean River about 800 metres downstream from The Cowpastures Bridge, just downstream from the junction with Narellan Creek. Construction began in July 1908, with access to the weir being through William John Cranfield's (1855-1927) land and was completed by October 1908. At one time, the weir was a popular boating venue. The weir was rebuilt after it collapsed in the late 1980s. (See Weirs).

CAMDEN WOOLLEN MILLS

Initially, the new Camden Steam building was a large three-storey building in Camden used to manufacture colonial tweed and woollen goods in 1885. The proprietors leased Henry Thompson's Flour Mill, thrown idle in 1863 by wheat rust, from his widow. In 1895 it traded as J.H. Gale and Co. A disastrous fire on 15 July 1899 destroyed the whole building and equipment. Operations were transferred to Bowenfels (Lithgow), and Camden lost the industry. (See Thompson's Steam Mill). The chimney stack was finally removed in 1971.

CAMELOT

Camelot is the property at 151 Kirkham Lane, a noted mansion on the western portion of the original Kirkham grant, between Kirkham Lane and the Nepean River. The mansion was built by The Hon. James White (1828-1890) and later owned by William Hugh Anderson (1869-

1912) and his wife, Frances Lillian Anderson née Faithfull. After her husband's death, the family was known as Faithfull-Anderson.

Camelot spans two grants, each of 1000 acres originally granted in 1815 to the Colony's Surveyor-General and explorer, John Joseph William Molesworth Oxley (1784-1828). The present house was built in the 1880s (the favoured date is 1888) for parliamentarian and racehorse owner The Hon. James White (1828-1890). Built by Canadian-born architect John Horbury Hunt, on the foundation of the old Kirkham Flour Windmill and later steam mill. When it was built, the house was referred to as Kirkham House, the name Oxley chose for the land granted to him. Oxley's house Kirkham is believed to have stood in the kitchen garden of the Camelot Estate. Anderson's wife Frances gave the house its current name - Camelot. When she first saw the house, she is said to have remarked it reminded her of the ballad called The Lady of Shalot by Lord Alfred Tennyson — "the towers of fair Camelot."

CAMELOT GARDENER'S LODGE

Located at 151 Macquarie Grove Road, Kirkham, corner of Kirkham Lane, it is believed Hunt also built the two-storey cottage several years before Camelot. It has a timber verandah on the two northern corners. The steeply pitched roof has its original diamond pattern shingles. Other distinctive external features are the massive brick chimneys, and the timber trussed gable ends. In later years, the cottage was occupied by Camelot's gardener.

CAMPBELL PARK   Map 12–3

A grant of 220 acres in 1818 (Portion 19, Parish of Cook) to John Thomas Campbell (1770-1830), located at Bringelly.

CAMPBELLS FORD

Also known as The Ford, a Nepean River crossing on the track from Theresa Park to Wallacia and Mulgoa is downstream from Mount Hunter Rivulet Weir. The ford was named after John Thomas Campbell (1770-1830).

CAMPERDOWN   Map 1–2

Property of 640 acres was purchased in 1832 by Commander Alexander Martin RN (1789-1864) at Theresa Park. Martin named the property after the Battle of Camperdown, which he took part in during the Napoleonic Wars. He was also present at the Battle of Trafalgar.

CARINYA

A large single-storey house at 39 Menangle Road, Camden, was built in the 1920s by John Peat (1864-1955). The home of George Victor Sidman (1879-1953) and Alice Gertrude née Whiteman. Sidman was the proprietor of the Camden News newspaper and wrote the local history book on the town of Camden.

CARLON TOWN

Patrick Carlon (1807-1883) was a convict who arrived in 1828. In 1835 he purchased 820 acres in the Burragorang Valley and, in 1840, received an adjoining grant of eighty acres (Portion 79, Parish of Picton). His property was known as Carlon Town, but it now lies beneath the waters of Lake Burragorang.

Alphabetical Place Names

CARNES FARM   Map 10–5

The farm was located on the grant of 700 acres in 1819 (Portion 34, Parish of Cabramatta) near Leppington to Thomas Carne (1787-1829). Carne was a Lieutenant in the 46th Regiment who had arrived on the Windham on 11 February 1814. In 1816 he married Mary Ann Broughton, the daughter of William Broughton (1768-1821), the Deputy Commissioner of NSW.

CARNES HILL - Leppington

A grant of 400 acres in 1816 to John Drummond (1808-1823), who added thirty acres in 1821. Carnes Hill was named for Thomas Carne (1787-1829).

CARPENTERS LANE

The original name for Elderslie Railway Station was after Horatio Carpenter (1827-1904), landowner. It was located near Macarthur Road, Elderslie. (See Railway/Tramway Stations).

CARRINGTON CENTENARY HOSPITAL FOR CONVALESCENTS

Carrington Hospital was a very important part of Australia's medical history, the first major medical facility built for convalescents in the Colony of NSW. Although officially opened in 1890, it was built in commemoration of the centenary of the Colony, which fell in 1888. It was named after the Governor of NSW (Robert Charles Carrington) at the time of the centenary. The land and funding of the Hospital came from a £10,000 gift from William Henry Paling (1825-1895) and an equal amount from the public and the NSW Government. It now forms part of the Carrington Retirement Village at 90 Werombi Rd, Grasmere.

CASWICK

(See Keswick)

CATHERINE FIELD   Map 10–6; 13–2; 14–1

A grant of 550 acres in 1817 (Portion 58, Parish of Cook) to George James Molle (1773-1823), soldier and Lieutenant Governor of NSW. The present location of Catherine Field Village was named after Molle's wife, Catherine.

CATHOLIC CEMETERY - Camden

The cemetery is at 150 Cawdor Road southwest of Camden, on the western side north of Burragorang Road. First known burials date from 1860. Several historical headstones were brought out of the Burragorang Valley.

CAWDOR   MAP 2–2; 4–2; 17–5; 18–6

A grant of 5000 acres in 1825 (Portion 11, Parish of Camden) to John Macarthur. The area between Camden and Razorback. The site of the first government station intended to catch the wild cattle of The Cowpastures. An early government Convict Settlement but a lack of permanent water is said to have prevented the development of a town at that location. (See Camden Park).

CAWDOR CEMETERY

The Uniting Church Cemetery on Cawdor Road was originally a Wesleyan/Primitive Methodist Cemetery. (See Uniting Church Cemetery)

CAWDOR ROAD

Now the road from Camden to Cawdor. It was part of the Great South Road crossing Razorback further on.

CAWDOR UNITING CHURCH

The church is the original Cawdor Methodist Church, built in the early 1800s. Around this, John Macarthur brought workers to Australia from England to manage and farm his extensive estates in the Camden area.

CHALKER'S COOL ROOM

Located on Portion 220, District of Camden, at the rear of the Cobbitty General Store 357 Cobbitty Road, Cobbitty. The Cool Room was built by William Chalker or Charker (1799-1880). It was still in use as a storeroom in 2019. It is heritage-listed. (See Cobbitty General Store)

CHANNELL'S FARM

A lease 1840-1860 on Woodbridge Road Menangle by William Channell (1811-1884), later taken up by his son William Channell Jr. (1833-1895). It was later farmed by Arthur Foot Onslow (1846-1919).

CHARLES FARM   Map 10–7

A grant of 700 acres in 1818 (Portion 32, Parish of Cabramatta) to Urban Fidkin (1768-1838), later owned by his son William Fidkin. In September 1891, the estate was purchased by Thomas Hussey Kelly, a Sydney-based merchant, and incorporated into a large subdivision known as The Cowpasture Estate and Cowpasture Farms.

CHELLASTON

The single-storey brick house is at 38 Menangle Road, Camden, north of Chellaston Street. The house was built by John Peat (1864-1955) as his own home. Later owners were Daniel Francis Maloney (1853-1937) and Charles Vyse (1911-1991).

Peat built many other houses in Menangle Road and elsewhere in the district.

CHERRYMOUNT

The property of John Dunbar (1821-1892) at Werombi was purchased in the 1860s.

CHESHAM COTTAGE

Located at 19 Elizabeth Street, Camden, it was the home of John Chesham (1867-1952) and his family. Later the residence of his daughter, Lillian May Chesham (1895-1956).

CHILDS FARM   Map 24–Lot 37

Originally the property of John William Childs (1874-1947). After WWI, an experimental agricultural farm and dairy were on the south side of The Oaks Road, Mount Hunter, halfway from Foster's Road and Westbrook Road.

Alphabetical Place Names

CHINESE MARKET GARDENS

There were six separate market gardens worked by Chinese men from Southern China along the Nepean River in Camden in the first half of the twentieth century. A display at the Camden Museum remembers their contribution to our local history.

CHURCH LANDS, THE

Robert Bruce Campbell donated the area of land in Hilder Street, Elderslie, to the Anglican Church (1859-1925). (See Hilsyde)

CHURCH AND SCHOOL GROUND

Eleven thousand four hundred twenty-eight acres (17 blocks along top of Razorback Plateau) were set aside in 1829 to provide funds for schools in Picton and Camden. In 1849 the blocks were re-released as annual rentals. The leases lapsed, and the land was sold in 1872.

CLARKSTONE   Map 19–2

Seven hundred eighty acres (Portion 19, Parish of Wilton) were purchased in 1835 by Captain William Henry Clarke, south of Moreton Park.

CLIFTON STATION   Map 6–3; 19–3

A grant of 500 acres in 1822 (Portion 15, Parish of Picton) to Thomas Cowper (1802-1883) on the south side of Razorback adjoining Apperl. In 1830 it was leased to the Church and School Lands Corporation.

CLYDEVILLE

The property of Reuben White (1861-1921) at Theresa Park.

COATES PARK - Cobbitty   Map 1–3; 15–2

A grant of 700 acres in 1812 (Portion 6, Parish of Cook) to Edward Smith Hall (1786-1860). A further 390 acres were added in 1817 (Portion 47, Parish of Cook). Colonel John Bruce Pye (1891-1963), who purchased the property in the 1920s, willed the property to the University of Sydney. In 2019 the property was part of the University Farm network and known as John Bruce Pye Farm. (See Halls Clear Ground)

COBBIDEE

The spelling was used in the 1860s. (See Cobbitty)

COBBITTY   Map 8–5; 9–4

Cobbitty Village is four kilometres north of Camden. The earliest reference to the name Cobbitty occurs in one of surveyor James Meehan's Field Books (Field Book, 69; Mitchell Library, Sydney). He mentions Coppety near the Nepean under the date 17 June 1809.

Gregory Blaxland mentions land at Cobbitty in a letter dated 1 June 1812. In his Tour of New South Wales, in October 1815, Macquarie speaks of the Kobbatty Hills. (See Cubbady)

COBBITTY CREEK

(See Sickles Creek)

Alphabetical Place Names

COBBITTY GENERAL STORE

A store located at 357 Cobbitty Road. At the rear is the heritage-listed building Chalker's Cool Room. The daughter of Albert Edward Vicary (1850-1933) paid for the construction of the present shop for Fredrick Leslie Small (1909-2002) when the old shop and house, which was further up the road, burned down in October 1941. The contents of the shop and house were only partially insured. The old general store had previously been the home of Hugh Campbell (1874-1944). Operated for many years by Joyce and Keith Thorn. (See Chalker's Cool Room)

COBBITTY PADDOCK/S

Cobbitty Paddock/s is an area of land on the south side of the Nepean River opposite Cobbitty Village and west of Camden Airport. It is now known as Ellis Lane. In 1853 a slab Methodist Chapel was erected on land opposite Corstophine, and in 1855 one acre was given to the Wesleyan Church. The building no longer exists. Cobbitty Paddock was one of the most vigorous farming centres in earlier days. It is in the vicinity of Brownlow Hill.

COBBITTY PARK

A grant of forty acres in 1819 in the Parish of Cook to Samuel Blackman (1819-1903) at 132 Cobbitty Road east of Windemere. Other owners include William James Rutter (1862-1916), Thomas Henry Mason (1862-1964) and John Gaunt.

COBBITTY RECTORY

(See St Paul's Rectory - Cobbitty)

COBBITTY WEIR   Map 7-4

Cobbitty Weir is a weir downstream from Cobbitty Bridge and Mt. Hunter Rivulet Weir and southwest of Cobbitty Village. It is upstream of Sharpe's Weir and the Nepean River's junction with Sickle's Creek. It has recently been rebuilt. (See Weirs)

COLDENHAM   Map 4–3; 5–3; 6–4

A grant of 900 acres in 1833 (Portion 137, Parish of Picton) to Major Henry Colden Antill (1779-1852) adjoining Jarvisfield near Picton.

COMMERCIAL BANK

The Commercial Banking Company opened in Sydney in 1860. The first Camden branch operated from the 1870s in a small shop front branch in Argyle Street. The shop was on the premises of Simpson's Tannery, which the bank purchased from Alexander Simpson (1817-1903). In 1878 the bank commenced a large and elegant building at 64 Argyle Street on the corner of John Street. (See National Bank). The original Argyle Street branch is now the site of the Camden Hotel.

COMMERCIAL HOTEL

Formerly the site of Ebeneezer Simpson's (1798-1855) tannery. Ebeneezer's son, Alexander Simpson (1817-1903), sold the site to Michael Page. In 1882 Charles Page (1840-1918) secured the site and built the Commercial Hotel. Later, the hotel was renamed the Camden Hotel. (See Camden Hotel)

COMMON, THE

The Common is an area of land off Cawdor Road south of the corner of Barsden Street, a gift of Elizabeth Macarthur-Onslow as an overnight campsite for teamsters. Frances Lillian Faithfull-

Alphabetical Place Names

Anderson and her daughter, Clarice Vivian, established a rest shelter for itinerant unemployed men there in the depression years of the late 1920s/1930s. It was a campsite for road workers and tarring gangs during the construction of the Hume Highway in the late 1920s. Also, the site of a Camden Council animal pound. The Camden RSL Youth Centre is now located here. (See Pound)

CONDELL PARK Map 19–4

Condell Park is a grant of 1920 acres in 1835 (Portion 1, Parish of Wilton) and 1280 acres in 1837 (Portion 15, Parish of Wilton) to Ousley Condell, a nephew of Major Gen. Sir Ralph Ousley. Condell named his property Condell Park, which was also given to a suburb of the same name. Mount Ousley is said to be named after him. At the present-day site of Douglas Park.

CONDRON CREEK

The creek on Camden Golf Course (Studley Park) was named after convict John Condron (1777-1833), a herdsman for Elizabeth Macarthur.

CONDRON FARM

A grant of 100 acres in 1812 (Portion 6, Parish of Narellan) to John Condron (1777-1833).

CONNOR'S FARM

A grant of sixty acres in 1811 (Portion 42, Parish of Narellan, east of Gledswood) to Owen Connor (17??-1870). Connor was a convict who arrived on the ship Marquis Cornwallis in 1796. The farm was later the property of James Chisholm and formed part of Gledswood—also known as O'Connor's Farm. (See Gledswood).

COOBATTI

(See Cobbitty)

COONAC

The house at 47 Menangle Road, Camden, was built for Albert Stevens Huthnance (1882-1980) and Alice Huthnance, née Bridgeman. Huthnance was a prominent house painter in Camden for many years. Alfred Bernard Whittington later owned Coonac.

CORSTOPHINE Map 24

Part of the North Cawdor Estate. The property consisting of lots 79 to 83, was purchased in 1882 by George Alexander Porter (1836-1897). It lay south of Cobbitty Bridge and became a prominent dairy farm in the district. Now part of the University of Sydney farms at 445 Werombi Road.

COTTAGE GROVE Map 9–5; 10–8; 11–2; 12–4

Cottage Grove is a grant of 600 acres in 1818 (Portion 21, Parish of Cook) to Charles Reid, a clerk in the Secretary's office. Later part of Kelvin Park. (See Kelvin Park)

COTTAGE VALE Map 11–3; 12–5

A grant of 600 acres in 1818 (Portion 22, Parish of Cook) to Thomas William Laycock (1786-1823). Later part of Kelvin Park. (See Kelvin Park)

COVENTRY   Map 13–3

A grant of 200 acres in 1812 (Portion 52, Parish of Cook) to Rowland Hassall (1768-1820), east of Northern Road, Bringelly, and north of Lowe's Creek—also spelled Conveny.

COW-DE-KNAVES   Map 10–9; 11–4

A grant of 700 acres in 1808 in the Parish of Cabramatta to Sir John Jamison (1786-1844), which he named Cow-de-Knaves. The name Cow-de-Knaves today refers to trig station TS10703 at Austral. (See Cabramatta)

COWPASTURES, THE

Cowpastures was an early name given by Governor Hunter in 1795 to the general area of Camden and Menangle—so named because it was the grazing area of the wild cattle which descended from cattle that escaped in the early days of the NSW Colony—also spelled Cow Pastures.

COWPASTURE ROAD

From about 1803, the road was from Prospect to the Nepean River. A road under this name still exists north of Leppington. From about 1830, the road south of Leppington was called the Great South Road. Now called Camden Valley Way. (See Great South Road)

CRAIGEND – The Oaks   Map 3–1; 4–4

A grant of 1280 acres in 1833 (Portion 9, Parish of Burragorang) to Thomas Inglis (1791-1872) south of The Oaks. His son William Inglis (1832-1896) had an adjoining thirty-two acres (Portion 42, Parish of Picton). The property was operated as a dairy and is still owned by the Inglis family.

CRAIGNAIR

Craignair is the two-storey white rendered brick house at 34 Menangle Road, Camden. Arthur Melville (Mel) Peat (1900-1982) built the house as his family home.

CRAIGYNOS

Craigynos is a single-storey house at 45 Menangle Road, Camden, built for Keith Whiteman and Marjory Whiteman, owners of the Whitemans Department Store in Camden.

CREAR HILL   Map 9–6

Crear Hill is a prominent hill in Harrington Park just east of the Northern Road. It was named after convict James Crear (1792-). Crear arrived as a convict in 1819 on the Baring 2 and worked for James Hassall at Bathurst in the 1823-1824 Convict Muster. In 1830 he was married to convict Mary West at Narellan by Rev Thomas Hassall. He later moved to the Lachlan region. His name is also spelled Crerar and Creaser.

CREAMERIES

Camden Park creameries were located at Camden, Mount Hunter, and Menangle. The Camden Park creameries produced the Laurel Brand of butter. Local farmers delivered their milk to the creamery, where it was separated. Creameries ended with the development of motorised transport in the early 1900s. (See Butter Factory)

Alphabetical Place Names

CROFTS HOTEL

The Woolpack Inn on the corner of Argyle and John Streets, Camden, was sometimes referred to as Crofts Hotel as Samuel Croft (1823-1906) was the publican. It was known as the Woolpack Inn from 1856-1864. A meeting place of Masonic Lodge until 1868. It was demolished for a new Bank of New South Wales building. (See Woolpack Inn)

CROWN HOTEL   Map 20 and 22

Located at 189 Argyle Street, Camden, near Murray Street, it was built in 1845 by Charles Waters (1818-1885). The publican in 1895 was James Edwin Waterworth (1858-1911). The hotel at that time was known as Waterworth's Hotel. By 1899 the Publican was Annie French, previously the publican of the Camden Inn. It has had several different facades over the years, including art deco and colonial (See Waters Hotel)

CUBBADY   Map 1–4; 8–7

A grant of 500 acres in October 1812 to Gregory Blaxland (1778-1853) on Cut Hill Road, Cobbitty. Almost immediately, Blaxland sold the land to Rowland Hassall (1768-1820). Rowland gave it to his son Jonathan Hassall (1798-1834) to add to his Matavai property next door. (See Cobbitty)

Cubbady is also a spelling variation of Cobbitty.

CUMMINGS FARM – The Oaks   Map 3–2

The name of the five hundred acres (Portion 63, Parish of Picton) was purchased by Patrick Cummings (1800-1878) and his sons John Cummings (1826-1881) and Benjamin Cummings (1832-1919). It adjoins Craigend.

CURRANS FARM

Property purchased by Michael Curran (1825-1918) at Currans Hill. Curran, born in Ireland, worked for a period at Glenlee.

CURRANS HILL

Location of the property of an early Narellan resident, Michael Curran (1825-1918), in the 1880s. Currans Hill Railway Station was located near what, in 2022, was the Catholic High School on Camden Valley Way. (See Railway/Tramway Stations)

CURTIS PARK   Map 10–10; 14–2

A grant of 1230 acres in 1815 (Portion 61, Parish of Cook) to Garnham Blaxcell (1778-1818) immediately south of Raby.

CUT HILL   Map 8–8

A hill 3 km north of Cobbitty in the centre of the Bosworth Farm was granted to Samuel Otto Hassall (1796-1830), and the grant of 230 acres in 1816, known as Freshfields, to James Hassall (1802-1862).

DAISY VALE   Map 4–5; 6–5

Portions 129, Parish of Picton and 131, Parish of Picton, owned by John Boardman at Picton. A dairying property.

DALKEITH

A single-storey brick house at 40 Menangle Road, Camden, was built for Charles Thomas Smart (1880-1952) from Menangle. Later owners were Harold Charles Henry Betts (1907-1986) and Robert John Picken.

DALRIEDA

The name of the large single-storey house at 41 Menangle Road, Camden, formerly named by Walter Charles Furner (1859-1939) as Pammenter. Later the home of Gerald Douglas Wylie (1900-1963) and Minnie Arthur Wylie, née McCaughney. (See Pammenter – Camden)

DAMS, THE

The Dams is the old name for Wetlands on Argyle Street, between the softball area and service station, near the Nepean River.

DANEFIELD

Property at Theresa Park, farmed by Lars Christian Hansen (1853-1936). The family came from Denmark.

DENBIGH - Cobbitty   Map 8–9; 9–7; 13–4; 15–3

A grant of 1100 acres in 1815 (Portion 44, Parish of Cook) to Charles Hook (1762-1826), who built a farmhouse. Adjacent to Netherbyes, west of Bringelly Road (now known as the Northern Road). Rev Thomas Hassall (1794-1868), the 'Galloping Parson,' purchased it in 1827 and built the two-storey portion. Charles Stewart McIntosh (1805-1875) and his descendants have owned the property since 1868. Renowned Ayrshire dairy stud until 1988.

DENHAM COURT

A grant of 500 acres in 1810 northeast of Ingleburn to Judge Advocate Richard Atkins (1745-1820). It was then purchased by Captain Richard Brooks (1765-1833). The historic Denham Court House is located at 238 Campbelltown Road, Denham Court.

DINNER CREEK

Halfway down the Burragorang Mountain. An important watering and camping site for teamsters.

DIXON'S FARM   Map 13–5

A grant of 3000 acres in 1816 (Portion 45, Parish of Cook) to John Dickson (1774-1843) (sometimes spelled Dixon) west of Northern Road, Bringelly, just south of Lowe's Creek. Later divided to become Maryland, Hill Paddock, and Rose Vale. (See Maryland, Hill Paddock, and Rose Vale)

DOCTOR CROOKSTON'S HOUSE   Map 20

Crookston's House is one of Camden's finest houses, located at 75 John Street opposite St John's Church. The Macarthurs built it for their overseer Robert Henry Druitt (1850-1899). This two-storey brick house, with its tennis court and brick stables, has been the home of several doctors, including Dr Robert Melville Crookston (1887-1977). Paul and Margaret Bowring later owned it for thirty-three years. Previously Dr William Hardy Jackson had lived in a house on this site.

DONOHUE'S CAVE

A cave on Flaggy Creek - Glenmore was reported to be a hideout of the bushranger Jack Donohue.

DOUGLAS PARK Map 19–5

A grant of 800 acres in 1822 (Portion 7, Parish of Camden) to Arthur Douglass, son of Henry Grattan Douglass (1790-1865). Now known as Douglas Park, it was initially known as Hoaretown. It is believed Douglass named the property after a prominent Quaker banker and friend Samuel Hoare. Later, the name was changed to Douglas Park at the residents' request.

DOUGLAS PARK WEIR

Located near Blades Bridge, the structure is a concrete fixed crest weir approximately 0.8 metres high and 40 metres across. A road causeway was added to the top of the weir structure.

DOVEDALE

Name given by George Caley (1770-1829) to the area now known as Bents Basin. Dovedale was named after a valley in Derbyshire, England. The name Dovedale is no longer in use. (See Bents Basin)

DOWDALL FARM Map 13–6

A grant of forty acres on 25 August 1812 (Portion 46 Parish of Cook) to Michael Dowdall (1776-1822). Dowdall had arrived as a convict in 1802. He drowned in 1822, and his widow, Eliza Cordelia Walker (1804-1835), a daughter of Rowland Hassall (1768-1820), became the owner. Her son Rowland Thomas Brisbane Walker inherited the property on 10 July 1835. Thomas Barker (1799-1875) and Joanna Barker, née Dickson (1800-1851) purchased the farm on 17 December 1855, which was then absorbed into the Maryland Estate. Sometimes spelled Dowdell. (See Dixon Farm, Maryland and Nonorah).

DRILL HALL Map 22

Now the A.H. and I. Hall (Agricultural, Horticultural, and Industrial), Argyle Street, also called the Show Hall, is part of the Camden Showground. It was built as a Military Drill Hall for the local NSW Mounted Rifle Detachment in 1894. They had an indoor target range that is now under the stage area.

DROXFORD Map 7–5

A grant of 100 acres in 1812 (Portion 19, Parish of Narellan) to Isaac Knight (1750-1842) on the Nepean River at Elderslie.

DRUITTS LANE

Druitts Lane is the former name of that section of Burragorang Road between the Old Hume Highway in South Camden and Cawdor Road. Edward Frederick Druitt (1856-1940) was a cordial maker operating his works on Burragorang Road and Cawdor Road corners.

EASTWOOD – Leppington Map 10–11; 13–7; 14–3

A grant of 1060 acres in 1819 in the Parish of Cook to Hannibal Hawkins Macarthur (1788-1861) bordered by Riley's Creek. Matthew Dysart Hunter (1803-1867) purchased the property and received an additional adjoining grant of 1040 acres in 1839.

EDITHVILLE

Edithville is a two-storey brick house at 18 Mitchell Street, Camden. Charles Furner (1824-1906) built the house and later lived in by his son Charles Furner Jr. The house was used as Camden's first hospital from April 1899 until 1902. Later used as doctors' rooms and owned by the Catholic Church. At one time known as Pine Villa. Extended and restored by Vaughan and Sue McInnes in the 1990s.

EDMONDSON – Edmondson Park

A grant of 410 acres in 1818 to John Drummond at Carnes's Hill, together with the purchase of part of the grants of 200 acres in 1819 to Robert Bostock (1784-1847) at Minto and 840 acres in 1819 to Henry Kitchen (1793-1842) an architect and surveyor at Minto. The property was purchased in 1906 by Joseph William Edmondson, a hotel proprietor from Campbelltown. Edmondson built a weatherboard farmhouse on the land known as Forest Home. Joseph William Edmondson (1883-1958), a farmer from Wagga Wagga, his wife, Maude Elizabeth Hurst (1885-1961) and son, John Hurst Edmondson, took up residence at Forest Home in 1916. John worked the property with his father until he enlisted in the Australian Imperial Forces during WWII. John was killed in action at Tobruk in 1941, leaving his father to manage the property alone. John was awarded a VC for his bravery.

EDROP ESTATE

Two hundred acres of the property of James Edrop (1793-1873) at North Menangle. Edrop had arrived as a convict in 1822. He also purchased land owned by Jeremiah Sullivan (1817-1864).

EL CABALLO BLANCO

El Caballo Blanco was a theme park established by Ray Williams at Catherine Field. Its main attraction was its Andalusian dancing stallions and Spanish-style architecture. The park also featured miniature Falabella horses and several non-equestrian-related amusements such as waterslides, train rides, and a small wildlife zoo. Formally part of the Gledswood Estate, the area is now a golf course and housing estate. (See Gledswood)

ELDER PARK

A grant of sixty acres in 1812 to William Charker or Chalker (1775-1823) at Bringelly along South Creek next to the 840 acres granted to Captain John Piper (1773-1851). He received a further grant of 125 acres in 1818. Charker, a convict, was later overseer of government stock at The Cowpastures, Cawdor.

ELDERSLIE   Map 7-9; 17-6

Elderslie is also spelled Ellerslie. A grant of 820 acres in 1816 and a further grant of 2400 acres in 1823 to John Joseph William Molesworth Oxley (1784-1828). By 1841 the land was owned by Charles Campbell (1810-1888), who planned a village and held a sale that year.

Harrington Street, Wilkinson Street and Macarthur Road were named at that time.

ELDERSLIE HOUSE

A house at 71 Macarthur Road was built by Johann (John) Bruchhauser (1820-1901) and later the home of his son Ernest John Bruchhauser (1890-1980). The Rev Edward Rogers (1812-1880) leased this home when he took charge of the Parish of St John's Camden.

Alphabetical Place Names

ELLENSVILLE

Property of John Edward Moore (1842-1916) between Mount Hunter village and Glenmore. Part of the old Hardwick grant to Hannibal Hawkins Macarthur. It contains a historic sandstone home.

ELLIS LANE

Named after Samuel Ellis (1850-1926), who farmed Fernleigh in Cobbitty Paddocks. (See Cobbitty Paddocks and Fernleigh)

ELMSHALL PARK

The estate of D'Arcy Wentworth (1762-1827). It consists of a grant of 1200 acres in 1816 (Portion 2, Parish of Cook), a grant of 1000 acres in 1816 and another grant of three hundred acres in 1819. Wentworth was a Medical Practitioner and Commandant/Supervisor of Convicts and one of those instrumental in establishing the Bank of New South Wales in 1816.

William Gore (1765-1845) also had an adjoining seven hundred acres known as Elmshall Park.

EMPIRE PICTURE THEATRE

The theatre was located at 147 Argyle Street for many years until the late 1950s. (See Royal Foresters Lodge)

ERRINGHI

The home of Edwin Frederick Lowe (1852-1917) and family during WWI at 15 Luker Street, Elderslie. Later home of William Adams (1886-1964) and Annie Linda Adams, née Auld.

ESKDALE   Map 7–7; 18–7

A grant of 3000 acres in 1818 (Portion 10, Parish of Narellan) to William Howe (1776-1855), which he named Eskdale. The property was later known as Glenlee. (See Glenlee).

EXETER FARM

Exeter Farm was a grant of two hundred acres in 1817 to Charles Gray, a former convict and later a clerk in the Secretary's office. At one time, a cottage known as Woodbine Cottage was located on the farm. James Badgery (1769-1827) and his son Andrew Badgery were associated with it. The farm was sold in 1853 to Thomas Roberts (1820-1906). The area is known as Badgerys Creek.

EXPERIMENTAL FARM

(See Childs Farm and Kirkham)

FAIRVIEW

Property of William Boardman (1801-1867) on The Old Oaks Road, Camden, that in 2019 remains in the hands of the Boardman family. It was on this property the early prize-winning wheat is reputed to have been grown by Jesse Dunk Jr. (1823-1896). Former piggery and later dairy cattle.

FAIRY HILL   Map 5–4; 6–6

Fairy Hill is a grant of 1000 acres in 1823 (Portion 134, Parish of Picton) to the merchant Philip Cavenagh. In the 1860s, the tenant was Ernest Louis Henry Royer (1832-1894).

FERGUSON'S NURSERY   Map 24

The nursery was started by Francis Ferguson (1824-1892), a one-time gardener to Sir Thomas Livingstone Mitchell and then to William Macarthur. The nursery was located at the northern end of Ferguson Road and was known as the Australian Nursery. It moved to Broughton Street in the 1930s, near the present ambulance station.

FERNHILL

A grant of 850 acres in 1821 to William Cox Sr. (1764-1837). His son, William Cox Jr. (1790-1850), built the house of that name c.1830.

The early name for Greendale.

FERNLEIGH

(See Ellis Lane)

FIRST HILL   Map 7–8

First Hill is a trigonometric station located at the highest point in Camden General Cemetery, Cawdor Road, Camden.

FLAGGY CROSSING - Glenmore

The property was owned by Robert Besting Moore (1820-1908) at Glenmore and recorded in 1850 as a stoney crossing place.

FLAGGY CROSSING – Picton

At the bottom of the steep hill on Old Razorback Road before the left-hand turn to join the new Razorback Road at the bottom of Razorback.

FLETCHER'S FARM   Map 7–9

A grant of forty acres on 10 June 1813 (Portion 22, Parish of Narellan) to Henrietta Fletcher, née Langley or Scriven (1787-1828) in Elderslie. She was the wife of Constable Edward Fletcher (1781-1856).

FLETCHER'S LOCK-UP

Police lock-up at Cawdor on the corner of Cawdor and Westbrook Roads, named after Edward Fletcher (1781-1856), the constable in charge in 1825.

FOOT ONSLOW BRIDGE

On Woodbridge Road, Menangle, between Menangle Road and the junction with Finn's Road, crossing Foot Onslow Creek. Named after Captain Arthur Alexander Walton Onslow's (1832-1882) cousin, Arthur Foot Onslow (1846-1919), who farmed here at Channell's Farm. (See Channell's Farm)

Alphabetical Place Names

FORD, THE

(See Campbell's Ford)

FORESTERS HALL

(See Royal Foresters Hall)

FRESHFIELDS   Map 15–4

A grant of 230 acres in 1816 to James Hassall (1802-1862) close to St Paul's Church, Cobbitty. Later, Andrew McKnight, the father-in-law of John Thomas McMinn (1843-1913), lived on the property. Later residents were George Willoughby Whatmore (1900-1958), Gordon Moffitt (1912-2002), and James Lingen Warrand. Moffitt was given the option to buy the property but declined, and he moved. The old entrance to Freshfields was at 229 Chittick Lane. Some locals knew Chittick Lane as Freshfields Lane and Moffitts Lane before officially being known as Chittick Lane.

GALVIN'S FARM   Map 7–10

A grant of forty acres in 1816 (Portion 17, Parish of Narellan) to Thomas Galvin (1788-1829) and his wife, Sarah née Wood (1782-1868) at 196 Macarthur Road, Elderslie. The historic house known as Galvin's Cottage is located on the grant.

Father Therry celebrated the first Mass in the area in Galvin's Cottage in the early 1820s.

GAMYAH

The single-storey brick house at 49 Menangle Road, Camden, was built by John Peat (1864-1955), once the home of Norman Thorn, engineer of Wollondilly Shire. It was later occupied by Sidney William Adams (1901-1980), manager of Whiteman's Store.

GASWORKS, THE

Located on Mitchell Street and demolished for the former old Camden High School. After remediation, the site is under development as the Camden Grove seniors living precinct.

GEORGE IV INN - Picton

The inn was built in 1839 by George Harper (1799-1841) at 180 Argyle Street on Abbotsford grant. (See Abbotsford)

GERMAN ROAD

So-called because German families lived there. The name was changed to Richardson Road, Narellan, during WWI.

GILBULLA

Gilbulla is an Arts and Crafts style mansion on the part of Camden Park, southeast of Menangle village at 710 Moreton Park Road, Menangle. Designed by Sulman and Power and built for Lt. Col. (later Major General) James William Macarthur-Onslow (1867-1946) in 1904. It became a Red Cross Hospital and was owned by the Anglican Church until 2002.

GLEBE – Camden

The area of church land surrounding St John's Church Camden. A part was sold in the late 1960s as the St John's Estate (Forrest Crescent). Similar church lands at Elderslie, Narellan, and Cobbitty. (See King's Bush)

GLEBE - Cobbitty

This glebe is an area of forty acres north of the Heber Chapel, Cobbitty, part of a parcel of land formally owned by James Greenwood.

GLEDSWOOD   Map 10–12; 14–4

Heritage-listed house located at 900 Camden Valley Way, Catherine Field, part of the property (400 acres) originally a grant to Gabriel Louis Marie Huon de Kerilleau in 1810 and was formerly known as Buckingham (Portion 45, Parish of Narellan). This historic property later included the grant of 170 acres to James Chisholm Sr. in 1818, known as Calder Farm (Portions 41 and 42 Parish of Narellan). Chisholm also purchased the grant of 500 acres to William Laycock (1784-1853) (Portion 46, Parish of Narellan). Chisholm renamed it Gledswood after Gledswood House on the Scottish border. Later, Anthony Hordern (1889-1970) and Feruccio (Frederick) Lino Testoni and his wife Theresa Testoni née McCullan established a farm tourism venue and commercial winery venture. By 2022 the estate was subdivided, and approval was granted to turn the house into a childcare centre. (See Buckingham, Laycock Farm and Calder Farm)

GLENDARUEL   Map 2–3

A grant of 2000 acres in 1823 (Portion 3, Parish of Weromba) to Peter Murdoch (1812-1896), south of Brownlow Hill, later added to the Brownlow Hill holding of Alexander MacLeay (1776-1848). Alternative spellings in the 1880s: Glendaroo, Glendarool, and Glenferrie.

GLENDIVER

A property of 800 acres at Glenmore was owned by James Gray Moore (1825-1889). James built the homestead of sandstone.

GLENDON

A home on the Brownlow Hill property off Brownlow Hill Loop Road.

GLENLEE

A grant of 3000 acres in 1823 to William Howe (1776-1855). Located on the eastern side of the Nepean River between Elderslie and Menangle. Site of a restored historic home. Howe arrived in 1816 as an Ensign with the 1st Royal Scots Regiment, later police magistrate, Justice of the Peace, Settler, Farmer, and dairyman. (See Eskdale)

GLENLEE WEIR

(See Bergin's Weir and Weirs)

GLENMORE

A locality between Mount Hunter village and The Oaks where Edward Moore (1790-1869) purchased 2000 acres of the estate held by Robert Johnston. The land was divided among Edward's three sons. Six hundred acres each to Joseph Moore (1814-1880) and Robert Besting Moore (1820-1908), who built sandstone homes for their families on this estate. James Gray Moore received the 800 acres called Glendiver. In 2019 Glenmore House is owned by Larry and Mickey Robertson.

GLENMORE UNITING CEMETERY

The Cemetery at 96 Moores Way, Glenmore, was established c.1867 as a Presbyterian Cemetery. The land for the cemetery was donated to the Presbyterian Church by George Frederick McDonald (1827-1879), a pioneer vigneron.

GLENMORE UNITING CHURCH

A Uniting Church at 96 Moores Way, Glenmore. Originally a Presbyterian Church.

GLENROCK   Map 1–5

A property at Werombi, owned by Jeremiah Hayter (1817-1891) and family, early settlers, who moved to the area in 1839 to work for the Macarthurs

GOVERNMENT HUT

Said to be the first dwelling built in the Camden district on the eastern side of the Nepean River at Elderslie. In 1805 a hut was built to store salt and equipment to catch the wild cattle. Constables John Warby (1780-1869) and John Jackson (1765-1840) were stationed there for a time. Its exact location is not known.

GRAHAMS HILL

On Camden Valley Way, Narellan, near the Narellan Hotel. The Camden to Campbelltown railway had a station at this location. It was named after John Graham (1816-1854), who farmed the area until the 1890s. Graham was the publican of the Queen's Arms Hotel, Narellan. (See Queen's Arms Hotel and Railway/Tramway Stations)

GRAHAM PARK   Map 9–8; 10–13

A grant of 2000 acres in 1815 (Portion 60, Parish of Cook) to William Douglas Campbell (1770-1827). Later known as Oran Park. (See Oran Park and Harrington Park)

GRASMERE

The name was used in the 1880s for William Henry Paling's (1825-1895) residence and property donated in 1888 to form the Carrington Hospital. Now applies to a residential area at that location.

It is sometimes misspelled as Grassmere. (See Carrington Convalescent Hospital).

GRASMERE COTTAGE

(See Carrington Convalescent Hospital).

GREAT SOUTH ROAD

The name was used from about 1830, for the road from the Nepean River along the present Cawdor Road and over Razorback Range which gave access to southern NSW.

Also known as Old Southern Road and the Port Philip Road. (See Old Razorback Road)

Alphabetical Place Names

GREEN HILLS, THE – The Oaks   Map 3-3

Part of the properties of The Meadow, Craigend and Victoria Park (Portions 8 and 9, Parish of Picton).

GREENDALE   Map 8–10; 16–2

A grant in 1811 of 500 acres (Portion 9, Parish of Narellan) to Mary Arabella Birch, née Forbes (1792-1882), which she named Greendale. Mary was the wife of Lieutenant John Birch, Paymaster for the 73rd Regiment.

GREENDALE HOUSE   Map 16–3

George Wentworth (1810-1851), a son of D'Arcy Wentworth, acquired the 1265-acre property known as Moulsey, previously owned by Ellis Bent (1783-1815) (Portion 11, Parish of Narellan) and built a home he named Greendale House. (See Mousley)

GREENS CORNER

Greens Corner is the name of the large WWII Army camp once located at the junction of Northern and Cobbitty Roads.

GRIMES' FARM

A grant of 335 acres in 1830 (Portion 35, Parish of Narellan) to George Grimes (1800-1854), east of Narellan and on the north side of Captain William Hilton Hovell's (1786-1875) Narralling grant.

GROVE, THE

An abbreviation of Macquarie Grove is applied to places nearby, particularly where Macquarie Grove Road crosses the Nepean River.

HAHNDORF

Property on The Old Oaks Road, Camden. Later known as Harben Vale in the late 1800s and early 1900s. (See Harben Vale)

HALLS CLEAR GROUND

A grant of 390 acres (Portion 47 Parish of Cook) to Edward Smith Hall (1786-1860) at Bringelly. Hall was the publisher of the Monitor (also known as Monitor). Later his holding included a further grant of 100 acres (Portion 6, Parish of Cook). This property was later owned by Colonel John Bruce Pye (1891-1963).

HAMPDEN VALE

The former property of Frank Hercules Dengate (1874-1951) and Mabel Victoria née Sheppard at Cawdor.

HARBEN VALE

Property previously owned by Timothy Willis (1809-1888) on The Oaks Road, Camden. A later owner was Edward John Lingen Crace (1915-2000).

Alphabetical Place Names

HARDWICK   Map 2–4

A grant of 2800 acres in 1840 (Portion 139, Parish of Weromba) to Hannibal Hawkins Macarthur (1788-1861), nephew of John Macarthur (1766-1834). Before purchasing the 2000 acres known as Glenmore, Edward Moore built a large sandstone house known as Hardwick. Shortly after World War II, the building burned down, and the ruin has since been removed. The shared boundary line between this property and Glenmore was Stoney Creek. The estate was later owned by Thomas Inglis (1791-1872). Also spelled Hardwicke. (See Ellensville)

HARRINGTON PARK   Map 9–9; 10–14

A grant on 10 June 1815 of 2000 acres (Portion 60, Parish of Narellan) to Captain William Douglas Campbell (1770-1827). Campbell named the property after his brig Harrington. Later owners were Abraham Davy (1809-1874), Thomas Rudd (1828-1899), Arthur Swan and Warwick Fairfax.

HARRINGTON PARK HOUSE

Harrington Park house is the historic house at 1 Hickson Circuit, Harrington Park. The house was restored as part of the Harrington Park development and, in 2019, is owned by the Fairfax family. (See Harrington Park)

HASSALL COTTAGE

Hassall Cottage is located at 101 Macquarie Grove Road, a farmhouse built about 1813 by Rowland Hassall (1768-1820). It preceded the building of the homestead of that name. Thought to have been the groom's cottage but later enlarged. The cottage is also known as Lucyville.

HEBER CHAPEL

Erected for Rev Thomas Hassall (1794-1868), it was the first church in the Camden district. The chapel was dedicated by Reverend Samuel Marsden (1765-1838) in 1828. St Paul's Church, Cobbitty, was built nearby.

HEBER VILLAGE

For a short period after the dedication of the Heber Chapel, the village of Cobbitty was known as Heber Village.

HEBERSHAM

The early name for Cobbitty Village was used by Rev Thomas Hassall (1794-1868).

HENNESSEY'S HOTEL

Hennessey's Hotel is a former name for Camden's Plough and Harrow Inn. It was known as Hennessey's Hotel in 1895 when the publican was Michael Laurence Hennessy (1855-1937). (See Plough and Harrow Inn)

HERBERT RIVULET

Herbert Rivulet is a creek on Camden Valley Way near Kirkham Lane. It funnels stormwater from below the Camden Bypass and feeds into Narellan Creek. (See Herbert's Hill)

HERBERTS HILL

A grant in 1814 of 100 acres (Portion 5, Parish of Narellan) to Thomas Herbert (1770-1846) between Narellan and Camden. Herbers Hill is also known as Rheinbergers Hill and Longleys Hill, later farmed by John Kelly Herbert (1835-1915). (See Rheinbergers Hill and Yamba)

HERMITAGE - The Oaks   Map 2–5; 4–6

A property of 857 acres was purchased in 1838 by John Henry Wild (1781-1834) (Portion 7, Parish of the Burragorang). This historic home is said to have been built by Rev Frederick Wilkinson (1796-1866), Colonial Chaplain.

HERZOG COTTAGE

The house is at 72 Macarthur Road, Elderslie, near the intersection of River Road. Once the residence of Anton Bernhard Herzog (1826-1908). Later the home of James Henry McDonagh (1862-1964) (postman), Joseph Pulling (1868-1940), John Gapes, and John Williams.

HILLCREST

The cottage at 7 Menangle Road, Camden, was built by John Peat (1864-1955) as a home. Fanny Rundle Hawkey (1864-1935) operated it as a boarding house around 1925. From 1936 the residence of Dr James Tatham Whittell Jefferis (1895-1972) and Ethel Rachel Ward Jefferis née Quinlan (1901-1992). A later owner was Walter Frederick Peters (1866-1928).

HILL PADDOCK - Bringelly   Map 8–11; 9–10

A grant of 294 acres in 1816 (Portion 45, Parish of Cook) to John Dickson (1774-1843) was originally part of the 3000-acre Dixon Farm grant. (See Dixon Farm, Maryland, and Rose Vale)

HILSYDE

Formerly a holiday cottage for Anglican Deaconesses at 59 Hilder Street, Elderslie, it was previously the historic house Pammenter. (See Pammenter – Elderslie).

HOARETOWN

The early name for Douglas Park. (See Douglas Park)

HOLZS WEIR

Holzs Weir is on the Nepean River, downstream of Cobbitty Weir. It was named for William Holz (1827-1894). In 2019 it was known as Mount Hunter Rivulet Weir. (See Mount Hunter Rivulet Weir and Weirs)

HOME FARM

The name given to the area of the first Camden Park buildings, including the cottage designed by Henry Kitchen (1793-1842) in which John Macarthur died—now known as Belgenny Farm.

HOP CHONGS

Formerly the site of a Chinese market garden at 3 Argyle Street, Camden, operated by Hop Chong (-1940), later a winery. In 2019 the location of the Italian restaurant building retained some elements of the old winery building plus the surrounding landscape has market gardens.

Alphabetical Place Names

HORATIO FARM

A grant in 1815 of 200 acres (Portion 38, Parish of Narellan) to William Mitchell (1786-1837), east of Molles Maine. Mitchell's wife (Elizabeth Broughton Huon Mitchell, née de Kerilleau) was the daughter of Gabriel Louis Marie Huon de Kerilleau (1769-1828).

HORSE AND JOCKEY INN

Formerly the home of George Taber Sr. at 170 Menangle Road, Menangle Park. Built c.1830 and intended as a hotel but later became the Taber residence. It reopened as a hotel in the 1860s.

Also known as Menangle House.

HOSKING FARM - Rossmore

A grant of 200 acres in 1812 (Portion 55, Parish of Cook) to John Edward Hosking (1806-1882), who was granted an additional 100 acres in 1819 adjoining his brother William Hosking's Perkham Farm and Shelley's Farm. Hosking, a merchant and later Mayor of Sydney, and his partner John Terry Hughes (1801-1852) became insolvent in 1843. They brought down the Bank of Australia, to which they owed more than £155,000. (See Perkham Farm and Shelley's Farm)

HOWEY FARM   Map 4–7; 5–5; 6–7

A grant of 1630 acres in 1814 (Portion 144, Parish of Picton) to John Werge Howey (1805-1871). The property was next door to Abbotsford.

HOXTON PARK

Hoxton Park was a grant of 800 acres in 1818 in the Parish of Cabramatta to Thomas Setrop Amos, a London solicitor who arrived in the Colony in 1816. Hoxton Park was named in 1887 when the Phillips and Co. syndicate subdivided the land under that name.

HUME HIGHWAY

A new road from Liverpool through Camden over the Razorback Hills was constructed about 1930. It became part of the Hume Highway, replacing the Great South Road. Later it was called Camden Valley Way, Argyle St, Murray St, Broughton St, Old Hume Highway and Remembrance Drive.

ICKLETON - Rossmore

A grant of 400 acres in 1818 Parish of Cabramatta to John Gurner (1792-1882) clerk to Barron Field, adjoining the estates of Barron Field (1786-1846) to the north and Henry Edward Marr (1770-1835) to the west. It was named after Ickleton, Cambridgeshire, England.

IDAVILLE

The house at 290 Cobbitty Road, Cobbitty, was once owned by James Robert Vicary (1860-1948) and Caroline Vicary, née Fryer (1857-1942) and later owned by their daughter Ida Elsie Mary Vicary (1891-1976) and her husband Charles Norman Cross (1893-1968).

IVY COTTAGE

This old home was on 361 Cobbitty Road until about 1955.

JACKSON'S FARM

A grant of forty acres in 1812 (Portion 30, Parish of Narellan) to John Jackson (1765-1840) on the north side of Mount Annan.

JAMESWOOD

A property at Mount Hunter that was owned by John Lunt Franklin (1846-1926) and his wives (first) Louisa Franklin née Biffin (1847-1882) and (second) Jane Franklin née Biffin (1853-1929).

JARVISFIELD   Map 5–6; 6–8

A grant of 2000 acres in 1822 (Portion 146, Parish of Picton) to Major Henry Colden Antill (1799-1852) on Remembrance Dr between Razorback and Picton. (Sometimes called Jervis Field). Jarvisfield is now called Antill Park Golf Club. It is named after Governor Macquarie's first wife, Jane Jarvis. Governor Lachlan Macquarie's estate in Scotland was also called Jarvisfield.

JOHNDILO

The property of John Stewart Rofe (1864-1930) and family west of Old Razorback Road, Cawdor. Formerly part of the Camden Park Estate.

JOHNSTON FARM   Map 2–6

A grant of 2000 acres in 1833 (Portion 2, Parish of Burragorang) to Robert Johnston (1792-1882), a son of Major George Johnston who was involved in The Rum Rebellion. Robert Johnston was elected as a magistrate in 1834.

KATHLEEN HAVEN

Kathleen Haven is a property with an orchard at 194 Cobbitty Road, Cobbitty, owned by McEvoy, who had a race track with the polo ground inside the track—later owned by Charles Henry David Wright (1915-1997) and Blanche Wright, née Greentree from the 1960s. The large interesting brick house was built for a former owner William Miller Dawson (1881-1955), and was named after his wife Kathleen Annie Gors (1882-1945). His brother, the famous baritone Peter Dawson (1882-1951), used to visit the property in the 1950s.

KEEWAYDIN

A weatherboard cottage at 72 Broughton Street, Camden, set back from the road. It was built in the late 1930s. Owners have been Gordon Hilder Butler (1909-1981) and Mabel Winifred (Poppy) Butler, née Richardson, and later Milton Brettell Ray (1926-2009), and Elaine Dawn Ray, née McEwan.

KELVIN PARK

A grant of 470 acres in 1815 to John Thomas Campbell (1770-1830) of what is now a historic property at Bringelly. Also known as The Retreat, the property later included the properties of Cottage Vale and Cottage Grove. Other owners include Alfred Kennerley (1811-1897), later the Premier of Tasmania, James McDonald (1788-1868), and Miss Lorna McDonald. The house was built about 1820 by Thomas Laycock Jr. (See Cottage Grove and Cottage Vale)

KENMERE   Map 1–6; 8–12

A grant of 600 acres in 1812 (Portion 17, Parish of Cook) to John Purcell (1773-1851), a Lieutenant in the 73rd Regiment situated west of Cobbitty. Purcell was Commandant at Newcastle and later Chief Constable at Penrith for a short period. Sometimes incorrectly spelled Kenmore.

At one time, the property of William Holz, who renamed it Marshdale—now known as Kenmere Charolais Stud at 25 Cut Hill Road, Cobbitty.

KENNY HILL

Originally known as Kenny's Hill, it was renamed Kenny Hill in 1893, located on Narellan Road between the water supply canal and the Southwestern Freeway (M5 freeway), now Hume Highway (M31). It was named after Dr William Kenny (1781-1846), who lived on the hill between Campbelltown and Camden. (See Railway/Tramway Stations)

KENT ROW

The row of houses at the end of Arndell Street, on Camden Park Estate south of Camden, east of Old Hume Highway, South Camden.

KESWICK

Once part of Freshfields, it is now part of Roseneath. Also incorrectly written as Kreswick and Caswick.

KINGS BUSH RESERVE

The area is adjacent to the Nepean River near Onslow Ave, easily accessible from the Nepean River Cycleway. The reserve was named after the Rev Cecil John King (1863-1938), the Rector of St Johns from 1891 to 1927. The area was once part of the St John's glebe lands. The glebe extended from the church down to the Nepean River. The reserve was donated to the community by St John's in the 1970s as part of their Forrest Crescent development.

KIRKHAM   Map 7–11

A grant of 1000 acres, 10 June 1815 (Portion 3, Parish of Narellan) to Lieut. John Joseph William Molesworth Oxley (1784-1828) on the east bank of the Nepean River towards Narellan. It was named after Oxley's birthplace in Yorkshire, England. When the November 1828 census was taken, John Coghill (1785-1853), master of the ship Mangles, had taken over the management of the property. Also, it was an experimental agricultural farm in the early 1900s. Later owners were John Norton Oxley (1824-1891), The Hon. James White (1828-1890), William Hugh Anderson (1869-1912) and Sir Frederick Sutton (1912-2001). Part of the property has been subdivided for housing as Kirkham Meadows.

KIRKHAM LANE

Kirkham Lane is the road from Cowpastures Road (now Camden Valley Way) to Macquarie Grove Road. Until the Northern Road from Narellan was constructed, Kirkham Lane formed part of the route north from Camden to the Penrith district. Hence in the early times, sometimes called Penrith Road. A railway station was located at Kirkham Lane and Camden Valley Way intersection. (See Railway/Tramway Stations)

KIRKHAM STABLES

These stables are believed to be the oldest surviving stables in Australia, built by a naval officer, Surveyor-General and explorer Lieutenant John Joseph William Molesworth Oxley's (1788-1824) grant of 1815. Oxley called the estate Kirkham after his birthplace in Yorkshire. The stables are all that remain of Oxley's original country estate.

The inscription of '1816' on the wall of the stables is commonly thought to be the year of completion. The original residence was across the road, and Camelot now stands where Oxley built his windmill. The stables are made from rendered brick and have two storeys. It has been consistently used as a stable through the years. The anchor near Oxley Cottage was once on the grounds to memorialise Oxley. The grave of Chester (1874–1888), who won the Melbourne Cup in 1877 and was owned by The Hon. James White (1828-1890) is in a paddock near the stables.

KOBADY

Kobady is Governor Lachlan Macquarie's spelling of Cobbitty in his diary of 1815.

LAMBE'S RETREAT   Map 7–12

A grant of sixty-eight acres in 1812 (Portion 20, Parish of Narellan) to Edward Lambe (1817-1897) on the Nepean River at Elderslie

LAGOON FLATS

Cawdor area west of Cawdor Road at Cawdor.

LANSDOWNE

A property formerly part of Windemere at 80 Cobbitty Road near the Nepean River. The two-storey weatherboard house was built by Alexander McCulloch (1833-1913) and later owned by Joseph Sandrone (1899-1986). It is now part of the University Farms.

LARKINS COTTAGE

(See Camden Cottage)

LAURIETON

The house at 55 Menangle Road, Camden, was built for Margaret Clara Watts, née Draper (1891-1971). Margaret was a war widow. Her first husband, Hugh Gritton Watts, was killed in action in France on 26-2-1917. Margaret married dentist John Llewelyn Hogg (1887-1948) at St John's C/E Camden on 18-10-1922. Later owners were Arthur Hamilton Milton Dunbar (1903-1980), and James (Jim) Wills.

LAYCOCK FARM

A grant of 500 acres in 1812 (Portion 46, Parish of Cook) to William Laycock (1784-1852). Laycock was the son of Quartermaster Thomas Laycock (1756-1809). After his death, the property was purchased by James Chisholm (1772-1837). (See Gledswood)

LE FEVRES CORNER   Map 7–13; 17–7

A location at the western end of Sheather's Lane, Camden. The junction of Werombi Road and Ferguson Lane. John Le Fevre (1807-1879) was originally in business in King Street, Sydney. He was an early carpenter/joiner/builder who worked on St John's Church and Camden's second Court House and Lock-Up. The current name is Yewens Corner, named after the family who lived there. (See Yewens Corner)

LEPPINGTON

A grant of 700 acres, on 5 April 1821 (Portion 5, Parish of Minto), to William Cordeaux (1792-1839), the Land Commissioner who was also a Director of the Bank of Australia. The grant is on Leppington Creek and is the site of the present village of Leppington between Liverpool and Camden.

LIMERICK

(See Redmire)

LINN FARM

Property of 212 acres (Portions 110 and 138, Parish of Weromba), purchased by Robert Linn (1818-1869), an early settler of the Werombi area. The farm was next door to John Terry Hughes' (1801-1852) grant of Theresa Park.

Also known as Linn's Bridge and Linn's Hill.

LITTLE SANDY

This shallow water swimming area is in the Nepean River at the foot of Chellaston Street. It was used for this purpose until the Camden Swimming Pool was built. Also, the location of a popular footbridge between River Road Reserve Elderslie and lower Chellaston Street, Camden.

LOMAR   Map 1–7

A purchase of 640 acres in 1834 (Portion 10, Parish of Weromba) by John Marden (1803-1858) at Werombi. Marden was buried under a peach tree on the property. The legend is that he was buried standing up.

LONG GULLY

The area on The Oaks Road from Picton leads up to Mowbray Park.

LOOMES FARM

One hundred sixty-eight acres (Portion 27, Parish of Weromba), owned by John Edward Loomes (1858-1931), and 168 acres (Portion 35, Parish of Weromba), owned by his father, William Loomes (1819-1899).

LOOMES HILL

Loomes Hill is the long hill between Glenmore and The Oaks. It was named for John Edward Loomes (1858-1931), whose father settled in the district in the 1830s.

LUCAS FARM - Rossmore   Map 11–5; 12–6

A grant in 1818 of 500 acres (Portion 23, Parish of Cook) to Penelope Lucas (1772-1836). Lucas had been Governess to John and Elizabeth Macarthur's daughters.

LYNN FARM

Property of William Boardman (1801-1867) in 1841. It became a dairy farm owned by Frederick Joseph Doust (1864-1900). Now part of the Camden Bicentennial Park.

MACALISTER - Picton

This property combines numerous grants and land purchased by Lachlan McAlister (1797-1855), a soldier, mounted police officer, explorer, and a magistrate. McAlister received a grant of 640 acres in 1813, a grant of 640 acres in 1836, grants of 1000 acres and 150 acres in 1837, and further grants of 2000 acres and 560 acres in 1838. He also purchased 640 acres in 1834 and 640 acres in 1836. His properties were at the head of Myrtle Creek near what is now Maldon, near Picton.

McAlister purchased a total of 2545 acres. His son Matthew McAlister purchased a further 4534 acres in the area between 1835 and 1840.

MACARIA

Macaria is the two-storey residence at 37 John Street, Camden. It was built for Henry Thompson (1820-1871), now owned by Camden Council. It showcases gabled windows and high chimneys. On April 20, 1855, Thompson, the owner of the Camden Steam Mill, added to his holdings by purchasing a half-acre allotment from the estate of Sarah Middlehurst (née Milford and previously Tiffin) for £656.5.0. Sarah was once the housekeeper at Camden Park. Sarah had purchased the property from the Macarthurs on November 6, 1846, for £36. The adjoining property, known as Camden Cottage, was also owned by Sarah.

In 1860, Henry started building an elegant schoolhouse on the part of the land known as Macaria. He intended that the building be used by the Classical and Commercial School opened by William Gordon (1815-1877) in 1857. However, this intention was thwarted when Gordon moved to the new homestead built at Macquarie Grove for Rowland Hassall.

The discovery of gold in western NSW and Victoria in the 1850s caused a labour shortage, and Macaria remained unfinished until 1871. Unfortunately, Henry was never to live in the new house as on July 29, 1871, he was kicked in the head by his horse and killed instantly.

For many years it was the home of Dr Francis William West (1874-1932). The building is said to be haunted.

It once formed part of Camden Council's offices and now houses the Alan Baker Art Gallery.

MACARTHUR PARK

Macarthur Park is the beautiful and peaceful Garden Park at 13-13A Menangle Road, Camden, on the corner of Park Street. The land was given to the people of Camden for passive recreation by Elizabeth Macarthur-Onslow in 1905.

MACQUARIE GIFT   Map 7–14

A grant of 600 acres on 25 August 1812 (Portion 1, Parish of Narellan) to William Charles Cowper (1807-1875). It was later known as Wivenhoe and Mater Dei. (See Wivenhoe).

MACQUARIE GROVE

A grant of 400 acres, on August 25, 1812 (Portion 2, Parish of Narellan) to Rowland Hassall (1768-1820), now 107 Macquarie Grove. From January 12, 1857, it was leased by William Gordon as the Camden Commercial and Classical School. Later owned by Henry Dangar (1796-1861), The Hon. James White (1828-1890), H. McKellar, Gerald Verner Maxwell (1877-1965), Percy Crossing (1865-1948), and William Pritchard (1857-1913) before Francis Arthur Macarthur-Onslow (1879-1938).

MACQUARIE HOUSE

A picturesque home at 56A Ferguson Lane, Camden, built by George Edward Ardill (1857-1945) in 1890 as Our Boys' Home and operated as such until 1945. Operated in the 1950s as the Macquarie Hydro Guest House under the management of Mrs J. Overall. Now a private residence.

Alphabetical Place Names

MALDON   Map 6–9

The site of a large cement works southeast of Picton. Before the cement works, lime was burned in this area to make mortar for local buildings.

MANILDRA

The home of Martin Thurn (1830-1852) and family at 60 Harrington Street, Elderslie.

MARR FARM - Rossmore

A grant of 1100 acres in 1823 (Parish of Cabramatta) to Henry Edward Marr (1777-1835) added grants of 100 acres in 1823, 56 acres in 1831, and sixty acres in 1831.

MARSHDALE   Map 1–6; 8–12

The property at Cobbitty of William Holz (1827-1894) and Jane Briton Holz née Chappelle in 1868, previously known as Kenmere. (See Kenmere)

MARYFIELDS

The Franciscan Monastery on Narellan Road, Campbelltown. The nearby railway station was formerly known as Rudd's Gate after Thomas Rudd (1828-1899), who had received a grant of fifty acres in 1816. (See Railway/Tramway Stations)

MARYLAND   Map 9–11

A grant of 721 acres on 20 June 1816 (Portion 45, Parish of Cook) to John Dickson (1774-1843) (sometimes Dixon) as part of his Dixon Farm property at 773 Northern Road, Narellan. Matthew Dysart Hunter (1803-1867) acquired the property on 15 August 1838. Six hundred forty acres of the property was acquired on 7 July 1836 by Thomas Barker (1799-1875) and Joanna Barker, née Dickson (1800-1851). The 640 acres passed to Thomas Barker's second wife, Katherine Heath Barker, on 21 April 1862, then to her son Thomas Charles Barker (1863-1940) on 21 April 1903. On 17 September 1940, it was acquired by Ninian Alan Thomson (1893-1952) and finally passed to his daughters Annette Lillie Thomson (1921-2009) and Elizabeth Gillies Thomson (1920-2006) in 1963. A historic home. (See Nonorah, Dixon Farm, Hill Paddock, and Rose Vale)

MASCOTTE

A home at 220 Cobbitty Road, Cobbitty, once belonged to Charles Clissold (1861-1889). Later owners were James and Mary Ann Small and Eric William Sutherland Spear (1913-1994). Later renamed Moindah.

MATAHLI CREEK

The creek drains from Cawdor through the Bicentennial Park and joins the Nepean River downstream of Macquarie Grove and upstream of Sharpe's Weir.

MATAHLI FARM

A property leased by George Coker - formerly Cuckow (1809-1862) from the Macarthurs. Located southwest of Camden.

MATAVAI FARM   Map 15–5

A grant of 200 acres in 1816 (Portion 8, Parish of Cook) to Jonathan Hassall (1798-1834) at 315 Cut Hill Road. It is named after a bay in Tahiti. The property was later developed as a model farm by Jonathon's fourth son James and later owned by Edward John Lingen Crace (1915-2000). The remains of a stone and timber barn are still visible.

MATER DEI

Name used for the Catholic school at Wivenhoe. (See Macquarie Gift)

MAY FARM

The property of George Alexander Porter (1836-1897) and his family was used for dairying in May Farm Road, West Camden. It sold to the University of Sydney in about 1950 and is now part of the University Farms.

MAYFIELD FARM

Charles Wesley Smart and his family owned this property at 380 Cawdor Rd (1842-1919). A historic home.

McARTHUR FLATS   Map 8–13

A grant of 700 acres in 1817 (Portion 5, Parish of Cook) to John Wentworth (1795-1853) at Cobbitty, on the east side of Coates Park Road.

MEADOW, THE   Map 3–7

A property at The Oaks, which at one time was the northern part of Thomas Inglis' (1791-1872) grant of Craigend.

MEDHURST VALE

A grant in 1835 of 100 acres (Portion 32 Parish of Menangle) and fifty acres (Portion 30 Parish of Menangle) to Thomas Taber Sr. (1764-1843) at Menangle Park. His son Thomas Taber Jr. (1827-1907) received an additional fifty acres (Portion 16 Parish of Menangle). Another son, George Taber (1800-1885), received fifty acres (Portion 36, Parish of Menangle). The combined properties became Medhurst Vale.

MELROSE – Camden

The home of Frederick Keith Whiteman (1900-1959) and family at 69 John Street, later the name of retirement units at that address.

MELROSE – Camden Park   Map 6–10; 19–6

A grant of 1150 acres in 1822 (Portion 9, Parish of Camden) to William Macarthur. (See Camden Park)

MENANGLE   Map 18–8

The present village is southeast of Camden and south of Glenlee. Alternative spellings in some early writings are Manangle and Manhangle. An Aboriginal word for swamp or lagoon. (See Riversford)

MENANGLE CENTRAL CREAMERY

Menangle Central Creamery is also referred to as the Camden Park Central Creamer. It is located on the southern portion of a large irregular parcel of land west of Menangle Railway Station, with road access from Stevens Road, off Station Street. (See Butter Factory)

Alphabetical Place Names

MENANGLE GENERAL STORE

The picturesque corner Store and Post Office at 2 Station Street, Menangle, built about 1904 by the Camden Park Estate, is a major part of local history and still provides a rich insight into our agricultural past.

MENANGLE HOUSE

(See Horse and Jockey Inn)

MENANGLE WEIR

Menangle weir is the first weir on the Nepean River upstream from the Menangle Bridge. Construction began in September 1902. The structure is a fixed crest weir constructed of sandstone bricks, approximately 3 metres high and 78 metres across. It is heritage-listed and has recently been repaired. (See Weirs)

MERINO TAVERN

(See Camden Inn and Royal Hotel)

METHODIST MANSE

The home at 28 Hill Street, Camden, on the corner of Broughton Street, was originally the Methodist Church's property. Now a private home.

MILE POSTS

An old English form of assisting travellers in knowing the distance to towns. Located at:

- Argyle Street, opposite Camden Vale Milk Depot.
- Broughton Street near Camden Hospital.
- Wooden post on Cawdor Road 100 metres north of Catholic Cemetery.
- Wooden post marking 2.5 miles along Cawdor Road, opposite Mayfield Farm.

MILL PARK

The property is below Loomes Hill, near The Oaks. Originally it had a water mill. Owned by John Roberts (1852-1899) and later by Clifford Clinch and Edith née Fyffe.

MILTON - Picton   Map 4–8; 5–7; 6–11

A grant of 1000 acres in 1823 (Portion 138, Parish of Picton) to Robert Crawford (1799-1848).

MITCHELL HOUSE

Located at 29-31 Mitchell Street, Camden, this two-storey terrace building was built around the 1880s by Charles Furner (1824-1906) as two separate terraces for his sons.

MODEL DAIRIES

The nine Model Dairies of Camden Park were located at various sites on the property. Each dairyman was responsible for his herd under the general management centred at The Home Farm (now Belgenny Farm).

MODEL FARM

The farm of Thomas Rapley (1831-1890) and family at Werombi.

MOLLES MAIN   Map 10–15

A grant of 1550 acres in 1816 (Portion 37, Parish of Narellan) to Lieutenant Governor George James Molle (1773-1823). Northeast of the junction of Old Hume Highway and Oran Park Road, southwest of Gledswood. It is also known as Molles Main Farm, once used by Tooths Brewery as a spelling paddock for their delivery horses. Now forms part of the suburb of Gregory Hills.

MONKEY CREEK

(See Werriberri Creek)

MONTPELLIER   Map 4–9; 5–8

A property on The Oaks Road, Picton, an 1850s wine-producing area owned by Donald McKinnon (1809-1892). The property had been leased by Thomas Brennand (1801-1858) until 1848, when he was declared insolvent. The property is named for James Busby's (1801-1871) collection of 437 cuttings from the Montpellier Botanical Gardens that arrived in Sydney on board the convict ship Camden in 1824.

MOOREFIELD   Map 9–12; 10–16; 13–8

A grant of eighty-seven acres in 1812 in the Parish of Cook to Thomas Moore (1762-1840) adjoining Rowland Hassall's (1768-1820) Coventry. Moore had arrived as a ship's carpenter and, in 1796, was the master boat builder in the Colony. Moore left a will stating that the rents and income from all his properties, including Moorefield, were to provide a fund to augment clergy stipends. Moore Theological College was named in his memory.

MORETON PARK   Map 19–7

A grant of 2000 acres in 1822 (Portion 6, Parish of Camden) to Jean Baptiste Lehimas de Arrietta (1774-1838) at Douglas Park. Later renamed Mountbatten. Also spelled Morton Park. (See Spaniards Hill)

MOUNT ANNAN

A hill now within the Mount Annan Botanic Gardens. It was probably named by William Howe (1776-1855) of Glenlee. Also, the name of a suburb of Camden.

MOUNTBATTEN

Formerly known as Moreton Park. (See Moreton Park)

MOUNT GILEAD

A grant of 1300 acres in 1821 and 300 acres in 1823 to Thomas Rose (1773-1837). The property and hill are several kilometres south of Campbelltown on the west side of Appin Road. Edmund Hume Woodhouse (1823-1875) purchased Mount Gilead from Walter Friend on 16 September 1867. The property was later owned by Major General Sir Denzil Macarthur-Onslow (1904-1984). The remaining stone windmill base is visible for many kilometres.

MOUNT HERCULES HOMESTEAD

The property on the Razorback Range was first purchased by John Tickner (1819-1875) and later named by Frederick James Dengate (1839-1901). Frederick's daughter Elizabeth Mary Doust née Dengate is said to have had Burnham Grove Homestead built to replicate her home.

MOUNT HUNTER   Map 17–8

The hill on the northwest end of the Razorback Range and the name of the village located northwest of the hill. The hill was formerly known as Westbrook, named after Governor Hunter, who visited The Cowpastures in 1795.

MOUNT HUNTER CREAMERY

Located at 175 Burragorang Road, Mount Hunter, the building was one of the Camden Park Estate Butter Factories. This building was owned by Edward Lavercombe (1871-1957) and his descendants from 1912 until the death of his daughter Clara Letitia Margaret Lavercombe (1909-2000). (See Butter Factory)

MOUNT HUNTER CREEK

Mount Hunter Creek is an alternative name for Westbrook Creek.

MOUNT HUNTER RIVULET WEIR   Map 7–15

Sometimes referred to as Theresa Park Weir. (See Weirs). The weir is downstream from Cobbitty Weir and Cobbitty Bridge and upstream of the reserve near Mount Hunter Creek Bridge. According to WaterNSW, the Mount Hunter Rivulet Weir is in its original location, most of the original fabric remains, and it has needed only strengthening and refurbishing. It is heritage-listed. Other weirs like the Cobbitty Weir, were rebuilt in slightly different locations (e.g., Cobbitty Weir),

MOUNT JENKINS

Part of the southern area of Mount Hunter in the 1860s.

MOUNT PRUDHOE

The highest point of the Razorback Range is now the radio towers' site. Originally named Mount Hunter by Governor Hunter c.1796, this name was transferred to the present Mount Hunter before 1813.

MOUNT TAURUS

Governor Hunter climbed this hill on Camden Park southwest of Menangle village on his visit in 1795. There is a stone cairn on the summit to commemorate this event.

MOUSLEY   Map 16–4

A grant in 1811 of 1265 acres (Portion 11, Parish of Narellan) to Ellis Bent (1783-1815) includes the area known as Bents Basin. George Wentworth later acquired the property and built a home he named Greendale House

MOWBRAY PARK   Map 5–9

Mowbray Park is one thousand acres (Portion 123, Parish of Picton), purchased by William Barker in 1876. It had previously been known as Seabright Park. A grand house in the Queen Anne style with a gatehouse at the main entrance to the road to Picton, now known as Barker's Lodge Road, was built in 1865 by William Barker Jr. The property was sold in 1905 to Frederick Waley (1860-1933) and Ethel Kate Waley, née O'Connor. (See Seabright Park)

MUDDY WATERHOLE

Muddy Waterhole is on the southern side of the road at Oakdale. Teamsters made it to water their horses. The cost of the construction was by collection from teamsters. The collector was Frederick Nixon (1852-1920).

MULGOA FOREST

Mulgoa Forest was the name for Werombi until about 1890. The Werombi School used this name up to the early 1900s.

MURRANDAH

Part of Camden Park. Name of the property and home built for Arthur John (Jack) Macarthur-Onslow (1873-1953) in what is now South Camden. Later occupants were Lt. Col. (later Brigadier General) George MacLeay Macarthur-Onslow and Violet Marguerite Macarthur-Onslow, née Gordon. It now forms part of the retirement village and nursing home.

Also, the name of the chief of the Burra Burra tribe from Burragorang Valley. (See Balwearie)

MYRTLE CREEK

Myrtle Creek is a creek and property between Picton and Tahmoor.

NANT GWYLAN

Nant Gwylan is a Welsh-derived name for the house and property at 33a Exeter Street. It was owned by Evan Alfred Davies (1865-1954) and Mary Fabert, née Richardson. Later owned by Llewella Hope Evan Davies OAM (1901-2000). (See Camden Town Farm)

NARELLAN   Map 17–9; 18–9

Narellan is the town four kilometres northeast of Camden. The early police lock-up was located there, also two hotels, the White Horse and the Queen's Arms and a school hall. Established before Camden (See Narralling)

NARELLAN CREEK

Narellan Creek runs from Harrington Park Lake to join the Nepean River upstream of Camden Weir.

NARELLAN GRANGE

A grant in 1816 of 700 acres to Captain William Hilton Hovell (1786-1875), a merchant sea captain and explorer. One time name of the area between Narellan and Curran's Hill. (See Narralling)

NARELLAN HOTEL

279 Camden Valley Way Narellan. Formerly the Queen's Arms Hotel. (See Queen's Arms Hotel)

NARRALLING

A grant of 700 acres in 1816 (Portion 32, Parish of Narellan) to Captain William Hilton Hovell (1786-1875) at Narellan was spelled Narralling on the parish map. According to Hovell, this was the Aboriginal name for the locality. (See Narellan Grange)

Alphabetical Place Names

NATIONAL BANK

The building was built in 1878 at 64 Argyle Street, corner of John Street, as the Commercial Banking Company of Sydney. This name can still be seen on the facade. One of Camden's most prominent and attractive historic buildings. (See Commercial Bank)

NAVIGATION CREEK

The creek runs from the lagoon near Finns Road through Camden Park and joins the Nepean River downstream from Thurn's Weir.

NELGOWRIE

Property on Macquarie Grove Road opposite Caernarvon. Owners have included Captain Willie Larkin (1870-1963), Rupert Tucker and Daniel James Cleary (1898-1970) and his family.

NEPEAN HOUSE

The historic house at 1-3 Mitchell Street, Camden, was built for Henry Bensley (1821-1858) c.1857 in Victorian Gothic Style. It has picturesque and colonial characteristics. Early owners included Dr John Bleeck (1824-1890), who was a doctor in Camden from 1855-1865, William Packenham (1826-1907) and his family, and Howard Carlyle Southwell (1899-1951).

NEPEAN RIVER

The main river of the Camden area is subject to occasional severe flooding. Part of the Wollondilly, Cox's, Colo, and Hawkesbury River system runs into the sea at Broken Bay near Palm Beach. It was named during the early exploration of the area after the then Secretary of State (England) Evan Nepean, a friend of Governor Arthur Phillip. The river creates the large flood plains around the Camden township.

NEPEAN TOWERS   Map 19–8

Purchase of 1250 acres in 1834 (Portion 2, Parish of Wilton) and a grant of 2560 acres in 1835 (Portion 3, Parish of Wilton) to Thomas Livingstone Mitchell (1792-1855), south of Douglas Park. Mitchell built the homestead in 1843. Later owners were Dr Richard Lewis Jenkins (1815-1883) and currently the Catholic Church. It is also known as Park Hall and St Mary's Towers.

NESBITT HOME

43 Macarthur Road, Elderslie home of Richard Johnson Nesbitt (1862-1891), a draper, and his wife Ada Harriet Galvin (1863-1931).

NETHERBYES   Map 9–13; 10–17; 13–9

A grant of 1600 acres in 1816 to Lieutenant Governor George James Molle (1773-1823) immediately west of Oran Park and adjacent to Orielton on the southwest side. It was at one time the location of the Oran Park racing circuit. By 19 September 1840, Samuel Blackman (1790-1843) had purchased Lot No. 1 of Netherbyes on the condition that he afford a run for the bullocks of William Whybrow (1776-1852) and the other tenants on the property.

NETTLETON'S FARM   Map 7–16

A grant of forty acres in 1815 (Portion 21, Parish of Narellan) to Joseph Nettleton (1781-1838) of Elderslie.

NEWSTEAD - Bringelly   Map 8–14; 9–14

A grant of 1000 acres in 1812 (Parish of Cook) to Robert Lowe (1783-1832). He received another grant of 500 acres in 1817 (Parish of Cook) and a further grant of 700 acres in 1819 (Parish of Cook). Then, a purchase of 300 acres (Portion 48, Parish of Cook). Newstead is part of the Birling property. (See Birling)

NONORAH - Bringelly   Map 9–15; 10–18

A grant of 3000 acres on 20 June 1816 (Portion 57, Parish of Cook) to John Dickson (1774-1843), sometimes Dixon. Matthew Dysart Hunter (1803-1867) acquired the property on 15 August 1838. Also known as Noo-Noora, Nonnora and Maryland. (See Maryland and Dowdall's Farm)

NOO-NOORA

(See Nonorah)

NORTH CAMDEN

A grant of 5400 acres in 1825 (Portion 12, Parish of Camden) to John Macarthur. (See Camden Park)

NORTH CAWDOR   Map 24

The early name for the area is now Camden and West Camden. The area was subdivided and sold in 1887.

NORTHCOT

A property on the eastern side of Ellis Lane, formerly owned by James Butchers Whiteman (1822-1858).

NORTHERN ROAD

Northern Road is the main road between Narellan and Penrith. The section from Narellan to Cobbitty Road was not constructed until about the 1840s.

NORTH ROAD

The original name of Narellan Railway Station. (See Railway Stations)

NRMA PICNIC GROUNDS

NRMA Picnic Grounds is the former picnic ground beside the Nepean River off Werombi Road near Mount Hunter Rivulet.

OAKDALE

Oakdale is a village several kilometres west of The Oaks. It was originally settled by some early families. Also, the name of Michael Blattman's (1815-1875) property on Burragorang Road.

OAKES

Oakes is an early 1800s alternate spelling of The Oaks.

OAKS, THE Map 3–8

The Oaks is a village west of Glenmore and south of Orangeville. It was named by John Henry Wild (1781-1834) because of the profusion of she-oaks growing in the area.

OLDHAM HILLS

Arthur Ebeneezer Doust and his family owned the historic cottage at 276 Cawdor Road, Cawdor (1886-1960).

OLD RAZORBACK ROAD

Now the name for the former Great South Road over Razorback from Cawdor.

ONSLOW PARK Map 20; 22

Onslow Park is the name of the Camden Showground and Recreation Ground. The Macarthur-Onslow family gave the land in memory of Captain Arthur Alexander Walton Onslow (1832-1882) following his death in 1882.

ORANGEVILLE

Orangeville is the area between The Oaks and Werombi. It was named because of the many orange orchards in the area.

ORAN PARK Map 9–8; 10–13

A house at 931 Cobbitty Road, part of the original Harrington Park grant of 2000 acres (Part 60 Parish of Cook) to William Douglas Campbell (1770-1827). The house was built c.1850 and is located on the north side of Cobbitty Road between the Old Hume Highway (now Camden Valley Way) and the Northern Road. Later owners included Thomas Barker (1799-1875), Edward Lomas Moore (1822-1887), Atwill George Kendrick and from 1974, The Hon. Lionel John Seymour Dawson-Damer (1940-2000), and Ashley Dawson-Damer née Mann. The house is sometimes referred to as Catherine Park House due to the Catherine Fields subdivision.

ORIELTON Map 9–16; 10–19

A grant of 1620 acres on 10 June 1815 (Portion 43, Parish of Narellan) to Edward Lord (1781-1859), a Lieutenant in the Royal Marines at 179 Northern Road. It was sold to John Dickson (1774-1843) in 1822. Later owners were John Theodore Perry (1802-1880), Alfred Augustus Russell Beard (1898-1957) and Warwick Fairfax. It was located east of Kirkham and west of Harrington Park on the Northern Road. In 1839, Lot No. 2 of Orielton, which consisted of 1040 acres, was purchased by Matthew Dysart Hunter (1803-1867). Recently extensively renovated.

OROOLONG Map 16–5

A grant of 550 acres in 1812 (Portion 8, Parish of Cook) to Samuel Fowler (1801-1878). This property included what is now the Greendale Post Office.

OSTENLEIGH

Part of Camden Park Estate on Old Razorback Road on the Cawdor side of Mount Hercules, it was a dairy farm purchased by Edward Joseph Dengate (1866-1944) and then John Stewart Rofe (1964-1930). (See Cawdor)

OXLEY COTTAGE

The Cottage at 46 Camden Valley Way Elderslie. It was built on land originally part of the 1000-acre grant made by Governor Lachlan Macquarie to John Joseph William Molesworth Oxley (1794-1828) in 1815 - Kirkham and 850 acres in 1816 - Ellerslie. Unfortunately, no record has been found of its original builder. It is a typical workman's cottage, likely dating from the 1890s as part of a row of similar cottages along the road into Camden.

The cottage is built from bricks, most likely made at the brickworks in the town of Camden. The original roof of wooden shingles can be seen under the eaves of the back verandah. There were separate outbuildings located beside a brick well. It is believed that Clarice Vivian Faithfull-Anderson of Camelot paid for the cost of connecting electricity to the cottage. She was known for her generosity, done quietly and without public attention. The house was known for some time as Curry's Cottage. It was once owned by Daniel Curry (1832-1918) and his family (although not the main farmhouse), after whom the adjoining reserve is named. The cottage is home to the Camden Visitor Information Centre. A memorial outside remembers John Oxley.

OXLEY'S FARM

(See Kirkham)

PADDY CLARK'S HILL

Paddy Clark's hill is on the northern side of Cobbitty Village. A quarry at this site was the source of the sandstone for the construction of St Paul's Anglican Church Cobbitty in 1842 and for the 1926 porch addition. It was named for convict Patrick Clark (1791-1843).

PADDY'S SWAMP

Paddy's Swamp was the location of the first school at Werombi. It was named for Paddy Ward, a tinker.

PALING'S DAM

At seven acres in size, this was the biggest dam in the district in the 1880s, on the Carrington Retirement Village property west of Ferguson Lane.

PALMER COTTAGE - Cobbitty

The name dates from 1842. The house fell down before 1844 when William Chalker purchased one acre from Rev Thomas Hassall. The site of the heritage building is called Chalker's Coolroom.

PAMMENTER - Camden

One of two houses with this name was once owned by Walter Charles Furner (1859-1939). Furner named this large single-storey house at 41 Menangle Road, Camden Pammenter, after the original house at Elderslie. (See Dalreida)

PAMMENTER - Elderslie

This name was attached to two houses owned by Walter Charles Furner (1859-1939) and Eliza Ann née Stimson at different times. Furner named the home at 59 Hilder Street, Elderslie Pammenter, after Eliza Ann Furner's mother's maiden name. The Hilder Street house, previously owned by James Hilder (1814-1901) and his family, was later renamed Hilsyde. (See Hilsyde).

Alphabetical Place Names

PANSY

Pansy is the affectionate name of trains that ran between Camden and Campbelltown. Passenger services ended in 1963, and the line closed and sold off by about 1969. One of the trains used and rolling stock are on display at the NSW Rail Museum at Thirlmere.

PARK HALL   Map 19-8

(See Nepean Towers)

PARROTT FARM

A grant of 100 acres on 1 January 1810 (Portion 7, Parish of Narellan) to William Parrott (1761-1824), shoemaker to the Macarthurs, on the southwest side of Narellan village, now part of the Studley Park Golf Course.

PASS, THE

A pass in the Wilton area allowed the crossing of the Cataract River to the coast.

PASSCHENDAELE

Property of Eric Essington Eagles (1920-2008) on Brownlow Hill Loop Road. Formerly owned by Timothy Ship (1837-1857).

PEACH TREE BEND   Map 4–10; 18–10; 19–9

Peach Tree Bend is also known as Peach Tree Corner. A sharp curve in the Old Razorback Road. The site of convict construction barracks during road building over the range in the 1830s.

PEAR FARM - Rossmore   Map 10–20

A grant of 550 acres in 1818 (Portion 34, Parish of Cabramatta) to Matthew Pear (1770-1824).

PEMBERTON FARM   Map 16–6

A grant of 700 acres in 1812 (Parish of Cook) to George Thomas Palmer (1784-1854) at Bringelly.

PENRITH ROAD

The original name for Kirkham Railway Station at Kirkham Lane. (See Railway/Tramway Stations)

PERKHAM FARM - Rossmore   Map 9–17; 10–21

A grant of 200 acres in 1819 (Portion 53, Parish of Cook) to William Hosking (1888-1861). Hosking, an English writer, lecturer, and architect, received a further grant of 100 acres (Portion 56, Parish of Cook), adjoining his brother John Edward Hosking's Hosking Farm and Shelley's Farm. (See Shelley's Farm and Hosking Farm)

PETTINGALL STORE

In the 1840s, a two-storey Store and Post Office was located opposite Kirkham Lane on Camden Valley Way at Elderslie and was owned by John George Pettingall. Pettingall was accused of stealing a cheque belonging to Sir Charles Cowper from a post bag. However, the case was dismissed due to a lack of evidence. Pettingall then sold the store to Joseph Thompson, whose sons Samuel and Henry ran the store until they moved the business to Camden.

PICTON

The present township was named after Sir Thomas Picton, with whom Governor Brisbane had served while fighting Napoleon. The locality was earlier named Stonequarry. (See Stonequarry)

PINES, THE

The property formerly owned by Mr and Mrs R. Berry at North Menangle was previously the property of Victor Edward Ibbetson (1904-1982) and his family.

PLANTATION FARM

(See Denbigh)

PLEASANT VIEW FARM

James Butler (1807-1888) purchased Pleasant View Farm at Spotted Gum Range from William Alfred Wheatley (1825-1893). (See Spotted Gum Hill)

PLOUGH AND HARROW INN

The hotel is at 75-79 Argyle Street, Camden. Built by Samuel Arnold (1811-1896) and first leased to Thomas Brennan (1813-1894). Later named the Argyle Inn but has now reverted to the Plough and Harrow. (See Arnold's Inn)

POLICE PADDOCK, THE

The early police paddock area was at the intersection of Murray and Broughton Streets. After WWI, Constable Casey's police horse was kept at 42 John Street, the site of St Andrew's Presbyterian Church. The last mounted Constable was Cornelius David Keaton. (See St Andrew's Presbyterian Church)

POMARE   Map 7–17

Pomare is a grant of 150 acres in 1815 (Portion 39, Parish of Cook) to Rev Thomas Hassall. Now, 352-356 Cobbitty Road, Cobbitty to the east of St Paul's Church. The house was built for Thomas Cummings (1835-1907), who operated it as a guest house. At one stage, it had a 9-hole golf course and, in 1952, was operated by David Malcolm Campbell as a guest house. Also known as Pomara map 7-17, Pommare, the Cobbitty property, is now known as Teen Ranch. Before Cummings built the house, he operated a guesthouse at 324 Cobbitty Road, also called Pomare.

PONDICHERRY

Pondicherry is the name of a farm located on the eastern side of the Northern Road to the north of Oran Park.

POPLARS, THE

Former home and property of Albert Arthur (Bert) Tegel (1908-1999) and Thora Haroldene (Peg) née Reeve at 240A Macarthur Road, Spring Farm. They operated Tegel Turkeys along with table chickens. Some of the new streets are named after some of their breeds.

POST OFFICE HOTEL

The Argyle Street Camden Hotel is next to the old post office. The Publican was Bridget Page, née Downey (1841-1900), the wife of Charles Page (1840-1918). It commenced operating in 1880 but closed in 1882 when Charles Page, having purchased Ebeneezer Simpson's Tannery, erected the Commercial Hotel at 105 Argyle Street, Camden. The Post Office Hotel was later demolished.

POUND, THE

The first Camden Council animal pound was located at about 9 Barsden Street in the early 1900s. It was relocated to The Common on Cawdor Road and later to the Camden Council Depot at Narellan.

PRESBYTERIAN CHURCH

(See St Andrew's Presbyterian Church)

PRIMITIVE METHODISTS' CHAPEL

A simple hall built in Oxley Street in 1859 has since been demolished. However, the foundation stone survives in the wall of the present Uniting Church's Wesley Hall on the corner of Mitchell and John Streets.

PUMPKIN HILL

It is in the Oakdale area on the eastern side of the road running from Oakdale to Mowbray Park.

PYRAMID HILL

Part of the Razorback Range was named by the 1790 exploration party of Captain Watkin Tench, William Dawes, and Surgeon George Bouchier Worgan.

QUEEN'S ARMS, THE

The hotel is located at 283 Camden Valley Way Narellan, which opened in c.1847. The first publican was John Graham (1816-1854), followed by his son John Joseph Graham (1838-1906). It was remodelled in 1937 by publican John Henry (Don) Byrnes (1881-1957), and it was then known as Byrnes Hotel, but by 1939 it was known as the Narellan Hotel. In the 1950s, the Publican was Russell Frank Donnelly (1927-2010).

RABY Map 10–22; 13–10; 14–5

A grant in 1812 of 500 acres (Portion 63, Parish of Cook) to Alexander Riley (1778-1833) at 1025 Camden Valley Way, Catherine Field. A further 3000 acres were added in 1816. Riley was a Wool pioneer. The property was later owned by William Moore (1828-1878). Following the death of William Moore, his widow Caroline and brother-in-law Albert Stephen Burcher were executors of his estate. The property was transferred to Arthur Barrington Moore in 1907 (lots 1 and 2). After the death of Caroline in 1913, the remaining lots passed to Albert Stephen Burcher (lots 3, 4 and 5). David Edward Mitchell (1890-1958) and his family later owned the property. The grant is remembered in the name of a suburb in Campbelltown.

RACECOURSE CREEK

The creek drains from the southwest side of Razorback through Brookside and Jarvisfield.

RAILWAY/TRAMWAY STATIONS

The railway stations on the now defunct Camden and Campbelltown line were called:
- Campbelltown - separate platform off the main train line
- Maryfield or Rudd's Gate - opposite the entrance to TAFE and University

- Kenny Hill - near the Water Race on Narellan Rd
- Curran's Hill - opposite the Catholic High School
- Narellan or North Road - where the newer part of the Narellan Town Centre now stands
- Graham Hill Road - behind the Narellan Hotel in Graham Hills Rd
- Kirkham or Penrith Road - Kirkham Lane near Camden Valley Way
- Elderslie or Carpenter's Lane on Camden Valley Way at the intersection of Macarthur Rd
- Camden - first in Argyle St, then in Edward St with extensive shunting lines

None of the stations or track remains except for a few embankments at Elderslie. A display at the Camden Museum shows the line route, pictures, and memorabilia.

RAVENSWOOD - Greendale   Map 16–7

In 1832 Henry Tudor Shadforth (1803-1892) purchased 640 acres (Portion 12, Parish of Cook), which he named Ravenswood. His father, Lieutenant Colonel Thomas Shadforth (1771-1862), subsequently purchased an additional 640 acres in 1835.

RAYLEIGH

The farm of Frederick Laurie Cranfield (1888-1920) and family at Cawdor.

RAZORBACK RANGE

Razorback Range is the prominent ridge and the high area between Cawdor and Picton. It was named because of its steepness in traversing it by horse and dray and later in early model cars. Road construction and maintenance are complicated due to unstable geology and land slippages in the general area.

REDBANK

Name for the southwest portion of Picton township.

REDGATE COTTAGE

An old home that used to be at 413 Cobbitty Road was the home of John Roach (1811-1891) and his family. Roach was previously known as de Rosa but changed his name by Deed Poll.

REDMIRE

Redmire is the property at 65 Cobbitty Road, Cobbitty, opposite Windemere, running from the Nepean River to Arendal. It was owned by Blackman and Dowle and later known as Limerick. Now part of the Sydney University Farms.

REED'S or REID'S CORNER   Map 18–11; 19–10

The corner of Woodbridge Road, Station Street and Menangle Road at Menangle is named for Isaac Reid (1829-1887). He held an 1862 lease from the Camden Park Estate for Upper Picton, Riversford. Reid, also known as Isaac Reed, had arrived in 1850 as an immigrant on the Maria. The name is no longer in use.

REEVE'S HOUSE   Map 20

Reeve's House is in Argyle Street, Camden, on the corner of View Street. It was built in 1889 for the prominent schoolmaster and Mayor of Camden, Henry Pollock Reeves (1831-1900).

RESTELLA - Cobbitty

Originally the site of a slab hut was built for William Carus Ainsworth (1842-1904) on his orchard. Later a rambling old weatherboard and fibro home at 269-271 Cobbitty Road, Cobbitty, was built around it by Herbert Kendall Brent (1881-1929) and extended as a guesthouse with a tennis court, later separated into flats. It was later owned by Frederick Keith Whiteman (1900-1959) but has since been demolished.

RETREAT, THE

(See Kelvin Park)

RHEINBERGERS HILL

At 168 Camden Valley Way Elderslie, it was named for Peter Joseph Rheinberger (1845-1924), who had arrived with his family on the Caesar in 1855. The hill is better known as Herberts Hill. (See Herberts Hill) Now parkland is managed by Council.

RICHFIELD FARM

Willie Larkin's (1870-1963) property at Cawdor.

RIFLE BUTTS, THE

The area was used first by the Camden Mounted Rifle Troop and later by the Camden Rifle Club. In the early 20th century, located near the junction of the Nepean River and Matahli Creek on the Macquarie Grove property.

RITCHIES HILL

A hill near the crossroads of May Farm Road and Fosters Lane off Burragorang Road leads to Mount Hunter. It was named for William Cochrane Ritchie (1881-1928).

RIVERSFORD

The name was used for Menangle from 1840 to the 1860s.

RIVERVIEW

Riverview is the name of the home at 167 Cobbitty Road, Cobbitty, a former creamery or butter factory. Owned 1911-1913 by Jane Smith, wife of Henry Smith, and later by Norman Thomas Hore (1902-1976) and family. (See Butter Factory)

ROBERTS HILL

Roberts Hill is a hill on the Denbigh property, Cobbitty. The quarry at this site was the source of the sandstone for the construction of the St Pauls Anglican Church steeple in 1842.

ROSEBUD FARM

Property of Charles Clout (1805-1885) and family at Cawdor in the 1880s.

ROSENEATH

Roseneath is at 303 Cobbitty Road, Cobbitty. It was formerly owned by Thomas Chittick (1856-1931) and his family and later developed as a horse breeding stud by Robert Watson. Robert added the property onto Freshfields. Some very successful horses were bred at Roseneath.

ROSE VALE   Map 9–18

Nine hundred seventy acres (Portion 54 in the Parish of Cook), once owned by John Dickson (1774-1843). On the north are Hill Paddock and Maryland. To the south by Denbigh at Bringelly, on the Northern Road. Originally part of Dixon Farm. (See Dixon Farm. Hill Paddock and Maryland)

ROSSLYN   Map 19–11

Rosslyn was a grant of 1150 acres in 1822 (Portion 8, Parish of Camden) to James Macarthur, located south of Camden Park. An alternate spelling is Roslyn. (See Camden Park)

ROSSMORE   Map 10–23

The present village to the east of Bringelly was originally named Cabramatta. There was a horse stud in the area called Rossmoor Stud, and to avoid confusion with the new suburb of Cabramatta, the village and surrounds became known as Rossmore (See Cabramatta)

ROTOLACTOR

Located opposite Menangle General Store, Menangle, the Rotolactor was a circular building with rotating machinery used for milking. The design allowed many cows to be milked at once. This location became a popular tourist attraction until the 1970s when it was sold and eventually partly demolished.

ROUNDHOUSE, THE

Unusually designed octagonal residence on Brownlow Hill estate on Mount Hunter Rivulet. Said to have connections with the early government stock stations used to catch the wild cattle—part of Glendaruel dairy.

ROYAL FORESTERS LODGE, THE

The Meeting Hall of a lodge of this name at 147 Argyle Street, Camden built in 1908. It became the Empire Picture Show theatre, the Downes Department Store, and the Retravision Electrical Store. In 2019 it was Treasures on Argyle.

ROYAL HOTEL   Map 20

At the corner of Argyle St and Elizabeth St Camden, it was originally the Camden Inn. It then became the Royal Hotel before being redeveloped and named the Merino Tavern. In 2019 it was again known as the Royal Hotel. (See Camden Inn)

RUBANUA

An old weatherboard house in Cobbitty Road beside Restella was built for Alfred Edwin Taplin (1863-1941) and his family. It was at one time the home of Frederick William Taplin (1810-1891) and a guest house run by Mrs Cutheland. NSW Governor Phillip Game (1876-1961) occasionally stayed there when in Cobbitty for the polo.

RUBYVALE

Rubyvale is a property just west of the bridge at Mount Hunter village.

Alphabetical Place Names

RUDDS GATE

Rudd's Gate is between Kenny Hill and Campbelltown, known later as Maryfields. The Camden to Campbelltown railway had a station at this location. (See Railway/Tramway Stations)

RUSSELL FARM – The Oaks Map 3–4

A grant of 1000 acres in 1838 Parish of Picton to Captain William Russell (1806-1866). Formerly in the Royal Navy, Russell had considerable land holdings, including this farm just north of The Oaks village. He later settled in the Hunter region and became a member of the Legislative Assembly.

SCIRPUS MERE

The name was given by George Caley (1770-1829) to the largest of the Picton Lakes. Unfortunately, the name is no longer in use.

SEABRIGHT PARK - Picton Map 5–9

Seabright Park is a grant of 1000 acres (Portion 123, Parish of Picton) to Daniel MacLaine Ross, a relative of Governor Lachlan Macquarie. The property was sold several times, but by 1876, it was purchased by William Barker, who renamed it, Mowbray Park. (See Mowbray Park)

SHANKAMORE Map 1–8; 8–15

A grant of 470 acres in 1811 (Portion12, Parish of Cook) to John Thomas Campbell (1770-1830), to which another 1100 acres were added in 1819. It is located south of Greendale and east of Bent's Basin. It is also spelled Shancamore and Shancomore.

SHARMAN'S SLAB COTTAGE

Located at 11 Stewart Street, Harrington Park, James Sharman is the former home (1858-1940) and his family. (See Struggletown)

SHARPES WEIR Map 7–18

Sharpes Weir is a weir on the Nepean River downstream from Cowpastures Bridge, just west of Camden Airport, east of Moorefield Lane, and upstream from Cobbitty Weir. It was constructed on Frederick George Rapley's (1900-1995) Farm. The weir was named for George Sharpe (1838-1919). The weir has recently been rebuilt. (See Weirs)

SHEATHER'S LANE

Sheather's Lane runs from the junction of Cawdor Road to the corner of The Old Oaks Road.

The lane derives its name from a clearing lease held by James Sheather (1821-1895) on the Macarthurs' land. Use of the name is known from 1860 to the 1880s. The western end was known as Le Fevre's Corner (named for John Le Fevre 1807-1879). The lane was a rough track until Frederick Joseph Doust (1864-1900) improved it by laying a metal road base and making a culvert to allow the lane to drain during wet weather.

SHELLEY'S FARM Map 9–19; 10–24

A grant of 400 acres (Portion 54, Parish of Cook) to William James Shelley (1774-1815) at Bringelly. It joined Perkham Farm, owned by William Hosking and Hosking Farm, owned by John Edward Hosking (1806-1882) and leased in 1887 by James Alexander Myles (1867-1950) and Charles Myles. Now the site of Rossmore School. (See Perkham Farm and Hosking Farm)

Alphabetical Place Names

SICKLES BRIDGE

The bridge where Werombi Road crosses Sickle's Creek. Said to be a misspelling of the German migrant surname Seckold.

SICKLES CREEK

Also known as Cobbitty Creek, it joins the Nepean River downstream of Cobbitty Weir. Said to be a misspelling of the German migrant surname Seckold.

SILVERWOOD

A former home and property of Leslie Charles William (Les) Smart (1895-1960) and his family on May Farm Road near Brownlow Hill.

SIMPSON'S TANNERY

Ebeneezer Simpson Sr. (1798-1855) and his son Ebeneezer Simpson Jr. (1831-1890) operated a tannery with a shop front on Argyle Street Camden. The tannery was purchased in 1882 by Charles Page (1840-1918), who demolished the premises and built the Commercial Hotel, which later became the Camden Hotel. (See Camden Hotel and Commercial Hotel)

SMEATON GRANGE

A grant of 550 acres in 1811 (Portion 31, Parish of Narellan) to Charles Throsby (1777-1828) at 1 Sedgwick Street, Smeaton Grange, between Narellan and Kenny Hill. In about 2000, Smeaton Grange House was made part of the new Magdalene High School, also spelled Smeeton.

SOUTH CAMDEN   Map 19–12

A grant of 1565 acres in 1823 (Portion 5, Parish of Camden) to John Macarthur. Known as Benkennie and Belgenny. (See Belgenny Farm)

SOUTHCOT

Property on the eastern side of Ellis Lane, formerly owned by Nelson Thomas Whiteman (1815-1884).

SPANIARD(S) HILL   Map 19–13

Location and property two kilometres north of Douglas Park, which perpetuates the memory of the Spaniard Jean Baptiste Lehimas de Arrietta (or D'arrietta) (1774-1838), the original owner of Moreton Park. The old homestead was demolished in the 1980s. De Arrieta received a grant of 2000 acres in 1821 and a further grant of 2000 acres in 1822. (See Moreton Park)

SPECTACLE POND or BELGENNY LAGOON

Spectacle Pond/Belgenny Lagoon is a small body of water in Camden Park, southeast of Thurn's Weir. Near and adjacent to the Long Pond, James and William Macarthur planted English oaks and elms. It was a popular spot for Macarthur family picnics and recreation. It is being rejuvenated by the present generation of the Macarthur family.

SPEED FARM - Cobbitty   Map 8–16; 15–6

A grant of 200 acres in 1816 (Portion 4, Parish of Cook) to William John Speed (1761-1838) adjoining McArthur Flats.

SPOTTED GUM HILL

The long hill between Mount Hunter village and Glenmore. (See Pleasant View Farm)

SPRING CREEK

The creek is located south of Mount Hunter village. Spring creek was named after the creek, a tributary of Mount Hunter Rivulet that runs through it. Part of a subdivision of Williamswood. The property of George Lambert Dunn (1868-1945) is said to be the oldest farm in this location.

SPRINGFIELD

The property of Thomas Cranfield (1846-1896) and family at Mount Hunter in the 1890s.

SPRING HILL

Property at The Oaks, originally owned by William Rofe (1823-1896). At one time owned by Baron Frederick Elliott von Frankenberg (1889-1950), a controversial figure during WWII due to his German ancestry. He was born in the USA to a German father and an Australian mother. A small dairy on the property was run for him by Walter Thomas Smith (1900-1973).

SPRINGS RESERVE, THE

An area on Springs Road, Elderslie, was used for dumping and treating night soil before the construction of the sewerage system.

St ANDREWS PRESBYTERIAN CHURCH - Camden

The church is located at 44 John Street. It was originally located at the corner of Edward Street and Mitchell Street, Camden until the property was resumed for a railway yard.

St BARNABAS' CEMETERY - Werombi

The Anglican Cemetery (Plot 91, Parish of Weromba) at Werombi's first burial was in 1853.

St BARNABAS' CHURCH - Werombi

Anglican Church at Werombi. After Werombi was settled in the 1840s until 1855, services were held on various farms in the area. In 1866, a wooden slab and shingle roof church was constructed from a single Blackbutt tree on the site of the present hall. In 1895 the larger weatherboard building was erected further up the rise and was dedicated on 8 May 1895.

St JAMES' CHURCH - Menangle

Anglican Church at Menangle. In 1871 services were commenced at Menangle in the old schoolroom. An appeal was launched for funds to build a church. By the time the foundations were laid in March 1876, more than £600 had been contributed. The architect is thought to be John Horbury Hunt (1838-1904), and the builder was J. McBeth. The cost of the brick building was £650.

The beautiful pyramid-capped tower and semicircular apse, decorated chancel and Sanctuary were designed by the renowned Sydney architects Sulman and Power and built in c1898 as a memorial to members of the Macarthur family, the gift of Elizabeth Macarthur-Onslow. A peal of bells was installed in the early 2000s. The building and site are heritage classified.

St JEROME'S CHURCH - Cawdor

The weatherboard Anglican Church was built at Cawdor as a church hall for a cost of £232 by local builders Hindes and Farindon and officially opened in July 1905. Electric power was connected in 1951, and the film Smiley was shot partly around the church in 1956. Services ceased in 1975, and the building is currently leased to the adjacent Cawdor Primary School. The building was restored around 2005.

St JOHN'S CEMETERY - Camden

Anglican Cemetery is in the Churchyard of St John's Camden. The first burial took place in 1845 and now has many historic graves.

St JOHN'S CHURCH - Camden   Map 20

The Anglican Church at Camden. The foundation stone was laid in November 1840. By 1842 the basic structure of the building was complete, and the steeple was clearly visible throughout the district. However, due to drought and subsequent financial difficulties, the church was not completed and consecrated until 1849. In 1874 the chancel was extended utilising bricks from the old steam mill. The bricks were a perfect match as the church and steam mill had been built using bricks from the brick kiln near the Cowpasture Bridge. The clock was added in the 1880s. With its steeple, the Church of St John's is probably Camden's most recognisable image. It is listed on the State Heritage Register, along with its surrounding land and cemetery

St JOHN'S PAROCHIAL SCHOOL - Camden

On 1 July 1850, the foundation stone for St John's Parochial School, at the intersection of Hill and Broughton Streets, was laid by Bishop Broughton. The schoolhouse was built with financial aid from the Denominational Schools Board but closed in 1879 when schoolmaster Henry Pollock Reeves (1831-1900) and all the pupils moved to the Public School in Camden. The site was sold on 4 December 1906 to Mr F C Whiteman for £300. The proceeds were used to construct a church Hall next door to the old school site. This new building cost £600. Later, on 3 February 1926 saw the placement of the foundation stone for the current Camden Masonic Temple Hall.

St JOHN'S RECTORY AND COACHHOUSE - Camden

The Rectory is located at 22 Menangle Road, Camden. The Rectory and Coach House were built in 1859 by James and William Macarthur at the cost of £1,000 on the most perfect site in Camden, not far from the church. The two-storey Rectory has an attached single-storey kitchen wing and shuttered twelve pane sash windows and French doors; the roofs are slate. In 1905 the Camden Park Estate gave the Rectory and six acres of land to the Anglican Property Trust (See Glebe).

The Rectory, which has both a State Heritage Listing and National Trust Declaration, was built to provide a residence for the third Rector, Rev Henry Tingcombe (1809-1874). The previous rectors lived in Elderslie House, Elderslie, and Rev Robert Forrest (1802-1854) had farmland on the river side of Purcell Street near the present caravan park.

Part of the coach house was demolished to make way for Forrest Cresent.

St JOSEPH'S NUNNERY

Adjoining St Paul's in Mitchell Street was demolished to expand the school in the late 1990s.

St MARK'S CEMETERY - Picton

Anglican Cemetery Picton. The first burial took place in 1856.

Alphabetical Place Names

St MARK'S CHURCH – Elderslie

Former Anglican Church at 33A Luker Street, Elderslie, was built in 1902 at the request of Archbishop William Samaurez Smith (1836-1909). It is now a private home.

St MARK'S CHURCH - Picton

St Mark's is Picton's Anglican Church, which was opened for worship in 1856, some fifteen years after the township had been surveyed. Edward Blacket, the diocesan architect, designed the church in 1848. The foundation stone was laid in 1850 by the second minister of the Camden Anglican Parish, the Rev Edward Rogers (1812-1880).

St MARY'S TOWERS

(See Nepean Towers)

St PAUL'S CATHOLIC PRESBYTERY   Map 20

The house at 24-28 Hill Street, Camden, was built around 1919 as a Catholic Presbytery (residence of one or more priests).

Sold by the Catholic Church in the 1960s, it has been restored several times and is currently occupied by a firm of solicitors. The original foundation stone was laid in 1919 and remained on the building.

St PAUL'S CEMETERY - Cobbitty

Anglican Cemetery, which surrounds the church, has been used since about 1830. Previous services were held in the homes of local Catholics. Heritage-listed. (See Heber Chapel)

St PAUL'S CHURCH – Camden   Map 20

Catholic Church on the corner of John and Mitchell Streets Camden was built by J B Elphinstone. The foundation stone was laid in 1859, and the church was consecrated later that year. A larger church and presbytery were added in 1987. The Sisters of St Joseph's nunnery adjoined the church in Mitchell St

St PAUL'S CHURCH - Cobbitty

Anglican Church at Cobbitty was consecrated in 1842 and has been in continuous use. A beautiful sandstone church designed by John Verge and John Bibb. It was built when the Heber Chapel failed to provide adequate accommodation for the growing community.

St PAUL'S CHURCH - Mount Hunter

Anglican Church at Westbrook/Mount Hunter. In 1878 a planked wooden building was completed at Westbrook and used as a Sunday School and for occasional services. Previously services were held at parishioners' homes in the Spring Creek-Westbrook area. The chancel was added in 1893. The church bell is on a tall post nearby.

St PAUL'S RECTORY – Cobbitty

A beautiful two-storey sandstone home at 335 Cobbitty Road, Cobbitty, was built for the Anglican Church in 1870 and designed by George Allen Mansfield. The first Rector, Rev Thomas Hassall, lived at Denbigh. The Cobbitty Rectory was built on land provided by Rev Hassall across the road from the church about 1870 for Rev Arthur Wellesley Pain. The current Rector lives there today after numerous additions, repairs, and updates.

St PETER'S CHURCH - Theresa Park

Former Anglican Church at Theresa Park. A wooden school church was built at Theresa Park in 1854 to serve the Brownlow Hill and Theresa Park communities. In 1886 the present St Peter's Church was built. The pulpit in the church was originally used at the old St John's Church at Parramatta. It was presented to the Heber Chapel (1828), adjacent to St Paul's Church Cobbitty, by Rev Samuel Marsden, who dedicated the chapel. Later the pulpit was given to St Peter's Church by the Rev Arthur Wellesley Pain of Cobbitty. The church was closed during the ministry of Rev John Barry Burgess and sold to the Evangelical Sisterhood of Mary (a Lutheran order) during the ministry of Rev Trevor Edwards. The Sisters still use the church and adjoining property for their work.

St THOMAS' CEMETERY - Narellan

Anglican cemetery 6 Richardson Road, Narellan, with the first burial believed to have taken place in 1828. Now owned and used by the Muslim Association for burials.

St THOMAS' CHURCH - Narellan

The former Anglican Church is at 1A Wilson Crescent Narellan. The lands for the church and cemetery were marked out by Surveyor Robert Hoddle in 1827. Still, little was done until the 1830s, probably due to the town's size and lack of community support. Finally, on 10 November 1839, the first church was officially opened. This building was to serve the Anglican community at Narellan until 1884 and became known as the School Church. Built by Rev Thomas Hassall, it was used as a weekday schoolroom and a Sunday church. The form of the 1839 building was a simple rectangle when built. It then had several additions, including the end bay with two gothic windows, the rendering to the walls to simulate stonework, a brick skillion wing to the west and an eastern verandah with closed-end storerooms. In 2019 this building was used as a photographer's studio.

In 1884 a new brick building was erected next door, but it has now been sold and is used as a Wedding Chapel. A new Anglican Church with the same name was built in Richardson Road, Narellan.

STARGARD   Map 5–10; 6–12

A grant of 1000 acres in 1822 (Portion 145, Parish of Picton) to Charles Ludwig Christian Rümker (1788-1862), a German astronomer of land on the west side of the Nepean River, on the assurance that he would devote his time to scientific pursuits. Brisbane, in a dispatch to Henry Bathurst, third Earl Bathurst, in November 1823, requested that the grant should not be confirmed beyond 300 acres because Rümker had completely broken his promise. Bathurst, however, refused Brisbane's request, realising that this would be a case of one man's word against another's if it were further investigated. Rümker received further grants of 1000 acres in 1828, 200 acres in 1833 and 1200 acres in 1842.

STATION MASTERS COTTAGE

The cottage was located at 23 Argyle Street, Camden, where part of the car park for McDonald's is now.

STEVEYS FOREST

A location just north of the village of Oakdale.

Alphabetical Place Names

STILTON FARM - Picton Map 5–11; 6–13

Portion 13, Parish of Wilton, owned by William Coull (1823-1889). Coull, a Scottish seaman, had arrived in 1855 and was later a storekeeper and postmaster for Picton.

STOKE FARM - Cobbitty

A grant in 1812 of 400 acres (Portion 40, Parish of Cook) to Rowland Hassall (1768-1820) adjoining Denbigh. Rev Thomas Hassall inherited it. Early maps refer to it as Stake Farm.

STONELEIGH

Stoneleigh is an early colonial farmhouse originally owned by Rev Thomas Hassall and his family at 309 Cobbitty Road, Cobbitty, opposite Cobbitty Public School. It was purchased by schoolmaster Thomas Chittick (1856-1931) when he retired and then later owned by his son Wilfred Thomas Chittick (1904-1961) and daughter Linda Muriel Chittick (1902-1993). The old home was demolished in the 1990s.

STONEQUARRY

The early name for the town of Picton as the town is located on Stonequarry Creek.

STONY CROSSING

(See Flaggy Crossing - Glenmore)

STONY HILL or STONY RANGE

A ridge on the south side of the private road of Camden Park Estate adjacent to Home Farm, east of McCall Avenue, was the place of several cottages in former times.

STRATHMORE Map 3–5

Part of the Vanderville grant to John Henry Wild (1781-1834) later subdivided 410 acres (Portion 174, Parish of Picton) property of John Edward Moore (1868-1931) on Waterfall Creek at The Oaks. It was later owned by Gordon Howard Conrad Sarina. It was a guest house operated by Mr McMahon in the 1930s.

STRUGGLETOWN

Struggletown is the heritage precinct in Narellan at the corner of Stewart Street and Sharman Close. It consists of a subdivision and a group of remnant buildings of varied character representative of Narellan's early development and historical fabric. The film Rats of Tobruk was partly filmed in the area. (See Sharman's Slab Cottage)

STUDLEY PARK

A grant of 100 acres was given in 1810 to John Condron (1777-1833) and a grant of 100 acres to William Parrott (1761-1824) at 52 Lodges Road, Narellan, purchased as one parcel of land in 1888 by William Charles Payne (1870-1960), who built a large and notable Victorian mansion south of the Camden Valley Way between Narellan and Elderslie. Later it became the Camden Grammar School. With the outbreak of WWII, the property was acquired by the Department of the Army and used as a training school for officer graduates from the Eastern Command. In 1950, a group of local golfers obtained a lease and constructed a golf course. The house was still owned and maintained by the Army and used as a training school. In 1972 Parrott's Farm portion of the estate was subdivided to provide new residential areas for Narellan. The Army sold the house to

Charles Northan in 1984. Northan left the house in 1984, and it remained empty until bought by the Moran family in 2008.

It was named after Studley Park near Rippon, Yorkshire. England. Due to debts, Payne was forced to sell the house to the architect Francis Buckle in 1891. Now known as Studley Park House, it is within the grounds of the surrounding golf course. It is listed on the NSW State Heritage Register.

SUMMER HILL   Map 3–6; 5–12

A grant of 1000 acres in 1839 (Portion 140, Parish of Picton) to Thomas Coulson Jr. (1801-1840), who had arrived in the Brampton in 1823. His father was Quartermaster Thomas Coulson Sr. of the 3rd East Kent Regiment of Foot (The Buffs).

TALLIMBA

A Tudor style two-storey house on Werombi Road opposite the Carrington Retirement Village, built in the 1940s. Used by the CSIRO and NSW Department of Community Services. Now a private home.

TALOFA

The dark brick cottage at 25 Broughton Street, Camden, was built by John Peat (1864-1955). Walter Wheeler (1864-1940) and Cecil William Clifton (1897-1938) were owners.

TEMPERANCE HALL

At 38 John Street, Camden, the hall was the Camden Temperance Society meeting place in the 1870s. In 1916 it was remodelled and became the Camden Fire Station which operated until the 1970s. Then it was used as a St Vincent de Paul charity shop. The building formed part of the expansion to the Camden Library & Museum in 2005 and is now used as multipurpose rooms. (See Camden Fire Station)

THERESA PARK   Map 1–9

A grant of 1184 acres (Portion 7, Parish of Weromba) to John Terry Hughes (1801-1852), location between Brownlow Hill and Werombi. A chapel was erected in 1857. Hughes also owned 640 acres (Lot 9, Parish of Weromba) and 640 acres (Portion 10, Parish of Weromba). With his partner John Edward Hosking, Hughes became insolvent in 1843 and brought down the Bank of Australia, to which they owed more than £155,000.

THERESA PARK WEIR

It is better known as Mount Hunter Rivulet Weir on the Nepean River downstream of Cobbitty Weir. (See Mount Hunter Rivulet Weir and Weirs)

THOMPSON'S STEAM MILL

The mill was built in 1859 by Charles Furner (1824-1906) for Henry Thompson (1820-1871). This was the largest building in Camden and was located at the Sydney end of the main street of Camden, east of View Street. Later used as a Woollen Mill, it burned down in 1899. It had a high circular brick chimney which was demolished in 1971. The entry wall is still visible next to the service station on Argyle Street. (See Camden Woollen Mill)

THORNLEA

Thornlea is the former dairy farm of the Kirkpatrick family at Narellan.

THORN HILL

The early name for Curran's Hill.

THURNS WEIR

Thurns Weir is the weir upstream from the Macarthur Bridge and downstream from Spring Farm Creek. Named for Philip Thurn (1850-1954) of Elderslie. It has recently been renovated. (See Weirs)

TRAM, THE

Locals referred to the Campbelltown-Camden railway as The Tram. (See Railway/Tramway Stations and Pansy)

TRAMWAY/RAILWAY

The line from Campbelltown to Camden opened in 1882 as a tramway. Taken over by the government Railways in 1889 and, after that, officially called a railway. It was officially closed on 31/12/1962. Last used with a special tram running on 1/1/1963. (See Railway/Tramway Stations)

TREVONE

Former property and home of Richard Hawkey (1836-1901) at 285 Woodbridge Road, Menangle, near Razorback.

TULWAH DOWRA

Tulwah Dowra is a home located on Picton Road, The Oaks. Anna Marie Houghan Dunn, née Luther, the wife of Charles Augustus Dunn (1843-1917), was photographed in front of the house with two of her children in 1890.

UNITING CHURCH CEMETERY CAWDOR

The buildings are located at Cawdor Road, Cawdor. (See Cawdor Cemetery and Cawdor Uniting Church)

UPPER CAMDEN   Map 17–10; 18–12; 19–14

Upper Camden is the name of a grant of 2750 acres in 1805 (Portion 3, Parish of Camden) to John Macarthur. (See Camden Park).

VACCARY FOREST

George Caley gave the name to The Cowpastures area (1770-1829) on his trip to the area in 1803. The name is no longer in use. A variation on the Latin word for a place where cows are kept or pastured.

VANDERVILLE   Map 2–7; 3–9; 4–11

A grant of 2000 acres in 1830 (Portion 57, Parish of Weromba) to John Henry Wild (1781-1834). The name for the area is now The Oaks.

VARROVILLE - Campbelltown

A grant of 1,000 acres in 1810 to Dr Robert Townson (1762-1827), scholar, scientist, and settler. Later owned by Charles Sturt (1795-1869), explorer, soldier, and public servant; James Raymond

(1786-1851), the Postmaster General; and Alfred Cheeke (1810-1876), a judge. Mt Carmel Catholic College is now located there.

VAROKO

The name of an interesting house at 9 Menangle Road, Camden, built about 1905 by John Peat (1864-1955) for local businessman Frank Leslie Woodhill (1875-1918) and Maria Louise née Pepper. Renamed The Spire about 2002. Opposite St John's Church.

VERDUNDALE

The property of Thomas Emanuel Perkins (1869-1938) and family at Cawdor. The house was built c.1917 and later owned by Alan Stuckey (1914-2008).

VERMONT   Map 1–10; 8–17

A grant of 1750 acres (Portion 1, Parish of Cook) to William Charles Wentworth (1790-1872), near Greendale, west of Bringelly, west of Westwood and bounded by the Nepean River and Bringelly Creek.

VICARY COTTAGE - Cobbitty

The site of a house built by William Chalker (1799-1880) or Charker on one acre of land purchased from Rev Thomas Hassall. The house was later replaced by one built by Albert Edward Vicary (1850-1933) after he retired from Westwood. It is near the site of Chalker's Cool Room, a heritage building now known as The Cob. (See Chalker's Cool Room)

VICTORIA PARK   Map 3–10; 4–12; 5–13

A grant in 1835 of 1280 acres (Portion 9, Parish of Burragorang) on Monkey Creek to Thomas West (1772-1858), later owned by son Obed West (1807-1891), 8 kilometres on the west side of The Oaks Road running to Picton.

WAR MEMORIAL

A World War One War Memorial at Macarthur Park Camden is used for Remembrance Day services. Remembrance Gates name those who served from the local area. Formerly used for Anzac Day services which are now held at the Bicentennial Park. (See Macarthur Park)

WATERS HOTEL   Map 22

The hotel at 189 Argyle Street, Camden, was built in 1845 by Charles Waters (1818-1885). Shown as Waterworths Hotel on a map and now the Crown Hotel. (See Crown Hotel)

WATERWORKS

The term describes the water canal which crosses under Narellan Road at Kenny Hill (or called Water Race.)

WATTLE CREEK

Wattle Creek is a mid-1800s subdivision in the Theresa Park area with access off Bob's Range Road.

WEEMALU

The home is at 181 Cobbitty Road, Cobbitty - east of Riverview. The house was built for Robert William Napper (1924-2013) and his family. Robert Rawlinson and his family were later owners.

WEERONA

Weerona is the brick house at 42 Menangle Road, Camden. It was built by John Peat (1864-1955) as an investment in the 1920s and purchased in 1930 by Clarence Herbert Cranfield (1881-1953) and Catherine Ann née Blow.

WEETALABAH

The single-storey brick house at 57 Menangle Road, Camden, was built by John Peat (1864-1955) for Alfred Cecil Poole (1881-1968) and Florence Rebecca née Ferris of the coach building business. Later the home of Owen Fendick Blattman (1913-2004) and Annie Emily (Nan) née Daniels, long-time President, and Secretary, respectively, of the Camden Historical Society. They named it after their flooded Burragorang Valley property.

WEIRS

Local weirs were installed at various points along the river to provide irrigation water for local industry. While still used, many are undergoing modifications to improve environmental flows and fishways. There were thirteen major weirs on the Nepean River, including nine in the Camden district, but one of the weirs has now collapsed. (See individual entries)

UPPER NEPEAN

- Pheasants Nest Weir is one of the original water supply diversion weirs managed by Water NSW.
- Maldon Weir is located upstream of the Suspension Bridge. The structure is a concrete fixed crest weir approximately 15 metres high and 40 metres across. Blue Circle Southern Cement Ltd owns it.

CAMDEN AREA

- Douglas Park Weir
- Menangle Weir
- Bergin's Weir or Glenlee Weir
- Thurn's Weir
- Camden Weir

SHARPE'S WEIR

- Cobbitty Weir
- Mount Hunter Rivulet Weir or Holz's Weir
- Brownlow Hill Weir

LOWER NEPEAN

- Wallacia Weir was originally built as a wooden weir for the John Blaxland (1769-1845) flour mill at Grove Farm. It is now a concrete arch-gravity weir approximately 5 metres high and 48 metres across; it is currently listed on the State Heritage Inventory.
- Penrith Weir, part of the Rowing and Kayak and Sprint Course.

WELLINGTON PARK   Map 5–14; 6–14

A grant of 1000 acres in 1833 of Portion 133, Parish of Picton to William Elyard (1771-1853), a Surgeon Superintendent on the convict ship John Bull. Property on The Oaks Road, Picton, was later owned by brothers Stanley Seaton Rae (1892-1963) and Thomas Howard Elwin Rae (1904-1959). Wellington Park was a long-time dairy that produced champion dairy cattle.

WENDOUREE

Property at 75 Cut Hill Road, Cobbitty.

WEROMBI or WEROMBA

Werombi is a town located north of Orangeville and south of Silverdale.

WEROONA

Weroona is the small property of the Barberie family at 92 Cobbitty Road, Cobbitty, between Windemere and the Nepean River.

WERRIBERRI CREEK   Map 2–8; 3–11

The creek runs through the western side of The Oaks into Warragamba Dam. A Tharawal (Aboriginal) name for the song of the willie wagtail. It is also known as Monkey Creek.

WEST CAMDEN   Map 17–11; 19–15

A grant of 2065 acres in 1818 (Portion 4, Parish of Camden) to John Macarthur. (See Camden Park)

WESTBROOK

Westbrook is the name of the early village, now known as Mount Hunter, until the late 1920s or early 1930s. Thomas Dawson (1820-1893) purchased the land here from the Macarthurs in 1860. (See Brooks Flat)

WESTWOOD   Map 1–11; 8–18; 15–7

A grant of 800 acres in 1838 (Portion 3, Parish of Cook and Portion 19, Parish of Weromba) to Hannibal Hawkins Macarthur (1788-1861) on Coates Park Road, northwest of Cobbitty.

WHITE HORSE, THE

An early Narellan hotel.

WHITE HOUSE FARM

Once a popular restaurant and wedding venue on the Hume Highway, South Camden. Demolished and redeveloped as a service station.

WIGNELLS HILL

The name was used for a hill at the top of Macarthur Road, Elderslie, near River Rd. It was named after William Walter Wignell (1843-1913).

The name is no longer in use.

WILLIAMWOOD Map 2–9; 4–13

A grant of 600 acres in 1840 (Portion 132, Parish of Picton) to John Benton Wild (1806-1845) on Spring Creek, Mount Hunter.

WILTON PARK Map 9–20; 12–7

A grant of 220 acres in 1818 (Portion 18 Parish of Cook) to Daniel Cubitt (1768-1831). It is located on Greendale Road at Bringelly.

WINDEMERE

Property at 100 Cobbitty Road, Cobbitty, was owned by Ben Heath (1894-1961) and Alice Florence, née Ward, in the 1920s-1930s. The house was built about 1927 for the Heaths, who operated it as a guesthouse. A later owner was Eric William Burge (1919-2003) and his family from the 1960s until the present. On 31 May 1930, the artist George Washington Thomas Lambert (1873-1930) died while visiting the property. It was the home of the NSW Polo Club in the 1930s and had a golf course, tennis court and horse-riding facility. At one time spelled Windamere. Spelling differs from the English Lake District town and Lake Windermere.

WINDMILL HILL

Windmill Hill is the early name for the site of Camden District Hospital. Before the hospital, there was a windmill used for grinding wheat. Another windmill was located at Narellan.

WINE BOTTLE

A replica of a wine bottle 6 or 7 metres in height, 1½ metres in diameter, steel frame tin-covered, advertising a wine brand (Penfolds), which used to stand on the eastern side of Hume Highway, now Camden Valley Way, one kilometre north of the Smeaton Grange Road junction.

WINE SHANTY or WINESHOP

The wine saloon at Oakdale on the south side of Burragorang Road before the junction of Barker's Lodge Road.

WINNOW DOWN

Winnow Down is the property at 6 Winnow Down Lane, Cobbitty, east of Arendal, with a house built about 1912. Original owners were Rev Thomas Hassall, then John Blackman (1843-1940), William Wallace (1867-1941), Leslie William Roy Wheatley (1880-1974), Anthony Hordern (1889-1970) and then Joseph Charles Gray (1841-1930).

WIRE LANE

The old farm lane from Old Hume Highway/Remembrance Drive, South Camden, to Cawdor Road is now partially closed. The current roadway is slightly north of the local government boundary between Camden and Wollondilly.

WIVENHOE

A grant of 600 acres on 12 August 1812 (Portion 1, Parish of Narellan) to Rev William Cowper (1778-1858), northeast of Macquarie Grove. Later owners include Sir Charles Cowper (1805-1875), Henry Arding Thomas (1819-1884), Captain Oswald Watt (1878-1921), and the Catholic Church as the Mater Dei Special School. (See Macquarie Gift and Mater Dei).

WODONGA

Residence at 43 Menangle Road, Camden, was built by John Peat (1864-1955) for Percy Charles Furner (1885-1968) and Emma Margaret née McCallum and family as a single-storey house. Later, a second storey was added in a mock Tudor style. Later owners have been Patrick Philip Sibraa and David and Lyndell Fuller.

WOLVERTON   Map 8–19; 12–8

A grant of 800 acres in 1815 (Portion 14, Parish of Cook) to Ellis Bent (1783-1815) at Greendale, west of Bringelly.

WOODBURN – MOUNT HUNTER

The property Cecil John Biffin (1897-1987) and descendants at Biffin's Road, Mount Hunter.

WOODBURN – PICTON   Map 5–15

Woodburn is one hundred sixty acres (Portion 1, Parish of Picton) and 560 acres (Portion 254, Parish of Picton) located on Crocodile Creek.

WOODLANDS   Map 1–12

Four hundred three acres (Portion 143, Parish of Weromba) were purchased by John Lakeman (1811-1869), south of Theresa Park. The historic home was later owned by Rupert and Rita Tucker and their family.

WOODSTOCK

Woodstock is a property on Cobbitty Road, Cobbitty west of the Macarthur Anglican School. Former owners include William Charles Chalker or Charker (1828-1910) and William James Rutter (1862-1919). Oscar Arnold Sallows (1908-1973) worked the dairy on the property for the McIntosh brothers. Max Tegel built the house on the property.

WOOLPACK INN   Map 20

Corner of Argyle and John Streets, Camden. Built in 1853 but only used as a hotel until 1868, when it became the new Bank of NSW building. The building and its garden took in John Street from the corner to the School of Arts and on Argyle Street to Ebeneezer Simpson's Tannery. This building was demolished in 1936 and replaced by the current building and allowing for the erection of additional buildings on Argyle Street and St Andrew's Presbyterian Church on John Street. It is now the Westpac Bank. (See Crofts Hotel)

WORGAN RIVER

The early name was given to the Nepean River by a group of officers exploring The Cowpastures area in August 1790. The river was named after Surgeon George Bouchier Worgan (1757-1838), a member of the party and surgeon on the Sirius in the First Fleet.

WYEMBAH

House in Cobbitty Road between the Rectory and Chittick Lane. At one time, the home of Dugald Campbell (1825-1919).

YAMBA

181 Camden Valley Way Elderslie is the former orchard and property of Jack Longley (1918-1990) and Ellen Jean Longley, née Thomas, on the Old Hume Highway Narellan, opposite Studley Park. The house has been restored. (See Herberts Hill)

YARRAMAN

Yarraman is a grant of sixty acres in 1816 to William Marson. Marson received a further grant of forty-five acres in 1819. He was a former convict who had arrived on the Royal Admiral in 1800. The Clissold family owned the property on Cut Hill Road, Cobbitty, for many years. Later owners were George Norman Malcolm (1901-1988), Whiteman, Francis Andrew Farrell (1902-1965) and Raymond George Champion (1921-1998). The entrance is now at 249 Cobbitty Road.

YEWEN'S CORNER   Map 7–13

Yewen's Corner was originally known as Le Fevres Corner, located at the corner of Sheathers Lane and The Old Oaks Road, Camden. John Yewen (1905-1954) and Elizabeth née Arlow, Scottish immigrants, were residents from 1928 to 1950. When the Yewens moved, the building was demolished, and a plaque now marks the location. (See Le Fevres Corner).

Parish Map Locations

Maps provide a visual reference to the location of the many places and properties mentioned. While many locations can be found with Google, others cannot be so identified. Old parish or district maps show the land grants and properties' location, size, and the original owners' names. Camden is currently the fastest-growing local government area in NSW. These properties are disappearing, their names are changing, and in time they will become part of the Street Maps of Greater Sydney and forgotten.

It is hoped the following maps will assist family historians in identifying where their forebears lived and farmed. In some instances, District Maps only give an overall view of the area. A reference to a more detailed map is therefore given. For example, an area of the Cook Map appears to show the whole area belonging to Ellis Bent. In contrast, a perusal of a more detailed map of Bringelly clearly shows other properties and their owners.

By studying district maps, it was possible to identify property owners and properties not referred to in the previous edition of this book, for example, the intriguing Cow-de-Knaves. It also helped identify the reason for some place names. For example, Buggy Hill, in the Theresa Park/Weromba district. One may be forgiven for thinking the name refers to a horse-drawn vehicle and an incident that may have occurred on the hill, but it refers to the landowner Michael Buggy.

Online searches for properties give a modern-day view of a building or property.

Index to Properties

Place	Map	Location	Place	Map	Location
Abbotsford	5	1	Brisbane Farm	19	1
	6	1	Brownlow Hill	2	1
Anschau Farm	1	1		8	4
Apperl	5	2	Buckingham	10	3
	6	2	Cabramatta	9	3
Badgally Trig	10	1		10	4
Ballymacammon	8	1		11	1
	12	1	Camden	17	3
Bathurst Farm	12	2		18	3
Belmont	17	1	Camden General Cemetery	7	2
	18	1			
Bents Basin	8	2	Camden Park	17	4
	16	1		18	4
Bergins Weir	7	1	Camden Weir	7	3
Birling	9	1	Campbell Park	12	3
	13	1	Camperdown	1	2
Blomfield Trig	10	2	Carnes Farm	10	5
Bosworth Farm	15	1	Catherine Field	10	6
Bringelly	8	3		13	2
	9	2		14	1
Brisbane Farm	4	1	Cawdor	2	2
	17	2		4	2
	18	2		17	5

Parish Map Locations

Place	Map	Location
Cawdor	18	6
Charles Farm	10	7
Childs Farm	24	37
Clarkstone	19	2
Clifton Station	6	3
	19	3
Coates Park	1	3
	15	2
Cobbitty	8	5
	9	4
Cobbitty Weir	7	4
Coldenham	4	3
	5	3
	6	4
Condell Park	19	4
Corstophine	24	
Cottage Grove	9	5
	10	8
	11	2
	12	4
Cottage Vale	11	3
	12	5
Coveny	13	3
Cow-de-Knaves	10	9
	11	4
Craigend	3	1
	4	4
Crear Hill	9	6
Cubbady	1	4
	8	7
Cummings Farm	3	2
Curtis Park	10	10
	14	2
Cut Hill	8	8
Daisy Vale	4	5
	6	5
Denbigh	8	9
	9	7
	13	4
	15	3
Dixon Farm	13	5
Doctor Crookston's House	20	
Douglas Park	19	5
Dowdall Farm	13	6
Drill Hall	22	
Droxford	7	5
Eastwood	10	11

Place	Map	Location
Eastwood	13	7
	14	3
Elderslie	7	6
	17	6
Eskdale	7	7
	18	7
Fairy Hill	5	4
	6	6
	7	8
Fletcher's Farm	7	9
Freshfields	15	4
Galvin's Cottage	7	10
Gledswood	10	12
	14	4
Glendaruel	2	3
Glenrock	1	5
Graham Park	9	8
	10	13
Greeen Hills	3	3
Greendale	8	10
	16	2
Greendale House	16	3
Hardwick	2	4
Harrington Park	9	9
	10	14
Hermitage	2	5
	4	6
Hill Paddock	8	11
	9	10
Howey Farm	4	7
	5	5
	6	7
Jarvisfield	5	6
	6	8
Johnston Farm	2	6
Kenmere	1	6
	8	12
Kirkham	7	11
Lambe's Retreat	7	12
Le Fevre's Corner	7	13
	17	7
Lomar	1	7
Lucas Farm	11	5
	12	6
Macquarie Gift	7	14
Maldon	6	9
Marshdale	1	6
	8	12

Parish Map Locations

Place	Map	Location
Maryland	9	11
Matavai Farm	15	5
McArthur Flats	8	13
Meadow	3	7
Melrose	6	10
	19	6
Menangle	18	8
Milton	4	8
	5	7
	6	11
Molles Main	10	15
Montpellier	4	9
	5	8
Moorefield	9	12
	10	16
	13	8
Moreton Park	19	7
Mount Hunter	17	8
Mount Hunter Rivulet Weir	7	15
Mousley	16	4
Mowbray Park	5	9
Narellan	17	9
	18	9
Nepean Towers	19	8
Netherbyes	9	13
	10	17
	13	9
Nettleton's Farm	7	14
Newstead	8	14
	9	14
Nonorah	9	15
	10	18
North Cawdor	24	
Oaks, The	3	8
Onslow Park	20	
	22	
Oran Park	9	8
	10	13
Orielton	9	16
	10	19
Oroolong	16	5
Park Hall	19	7
Peach Tree Bend	4	10
	18	10
	19	9
Pear Farm	10	20
Pemberton Farm	16	6

Place	Map	Location
Perkham	9	17
	10	21
Pomara Grove	7	18
Raby	10	22
	13	10
	14	5
Ravenswood	16	7
Reed's Corner	18	11
	19	10
Rose Vale	9	18
Rosslyn	19	11
Rossmore	10	23
Rossmore School	11	6
Royal Hotel	20	
Russell Farm	3	4
Seabright Park	5	9
Shankamore	1	8
	8	15
Sharpe's Weir	7	19
Shelley Farm	9	19
	10	24
South Camden	19	12
Spaniard's Hill	19	13
Speed Farm	8	16
	15	6
St John's Church	20	
St Paul's Catholic Presbytery	20	
Stargard	5	10
	6	12
Stilton	5	11
	6	13
Strathmore	3	5
Summer Hill	3	6
	5	12
The Meadow	3	7
	3	7
The Oaks	3	8
Theresa Park	1	9
Upper Camden	17	10
	18	12
	19	14
Vanderville	2	7
	3	9
	4	11
Vermont	1	10
	8	17
Victoria Park	3	10

75

Parish Map Locations

Place	Map	Location
Victoria Park	4	12
	5	13
Walters Hotel	22	
Wellington Park	5	14
	6	14
Werriberri Creek	2	8
	3	11
West Camden	17	11
Westwood	1	11
	8	18
	15	7
Williamswood	2	9
	4	13

Place	Map	Location
Wilton Park	9	20
	12	7
Wolverton	8	19
	12	8
Woodburn - Picton	5	15
Woodlands	1	12
Woolpack Inn	20	
Yewen's Corner	7	13

Parish Map Locations

MAP 1 Parish of Weromba – map dated 19 December 1922

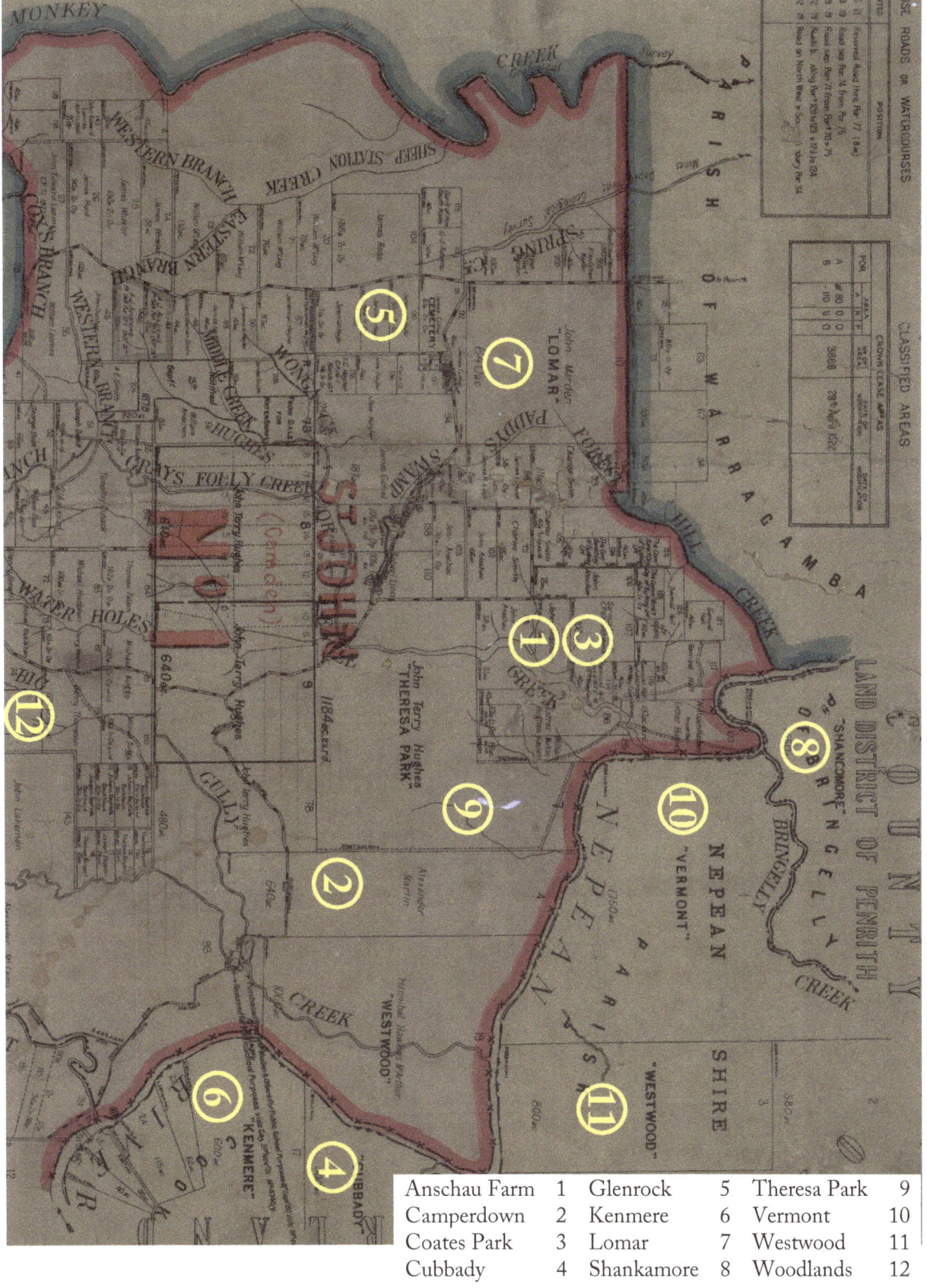

Anschau Farm	1	Glenrock	5	Theresa Park	9
Camperdown	2	Kenmere	6	Vermont	10
Coates Park	3	Lomar	7	Westwood	11
Cubbady	4	Shankamore	8	Woodlands	12

Parish Map Locations

MAP 2 Parish of Weromba - map dated 19 December 1922

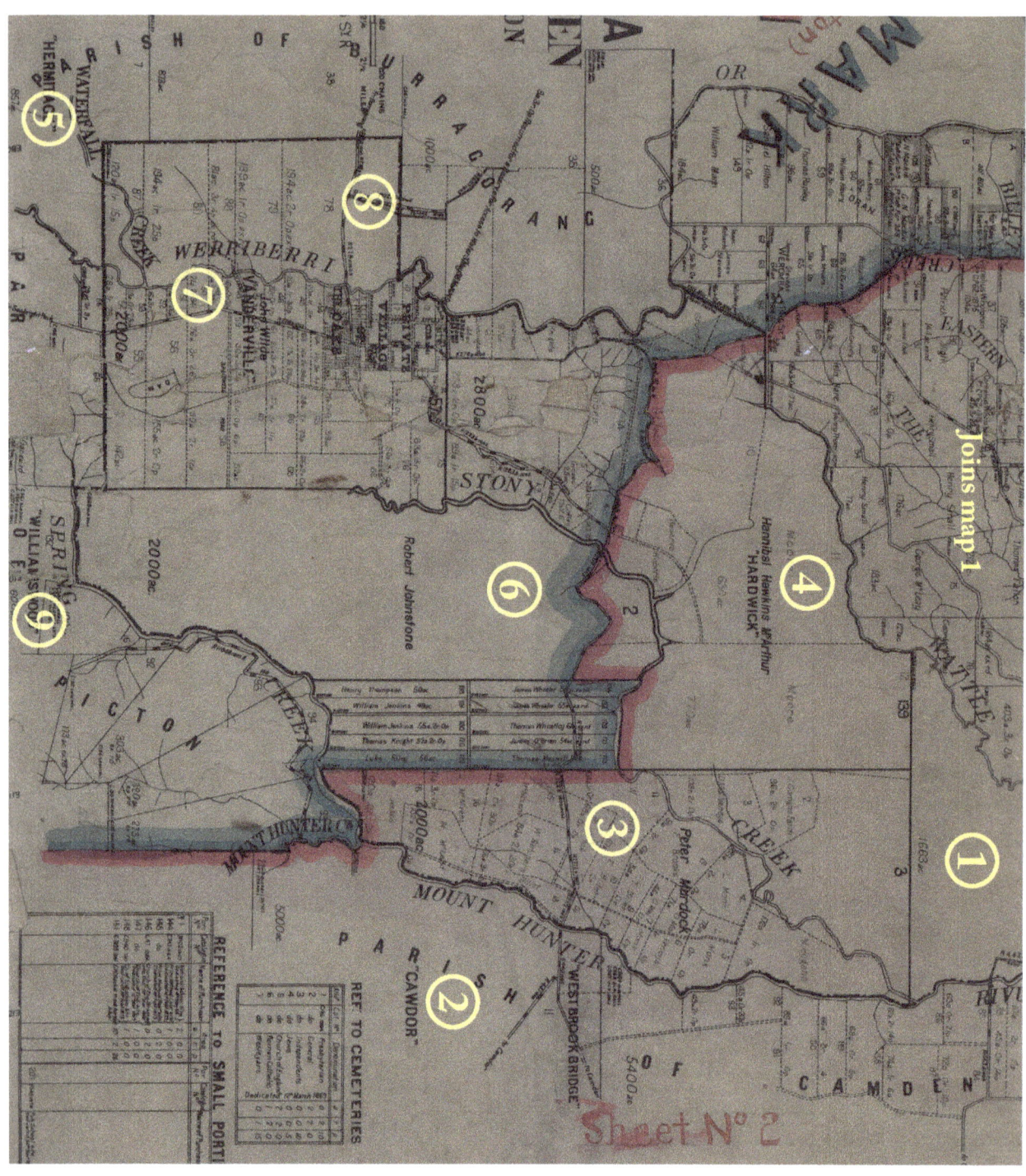

Brownlow Hill	1	Hermitage	5	Williamswood	9
Cawdor	2	Johnston Farm	6		
Glendaruel	3	Vanderville	7		
Hardwick	4	Werriberri Creek	8		

Parish Map Locations

MAP 3 Parish of Picton

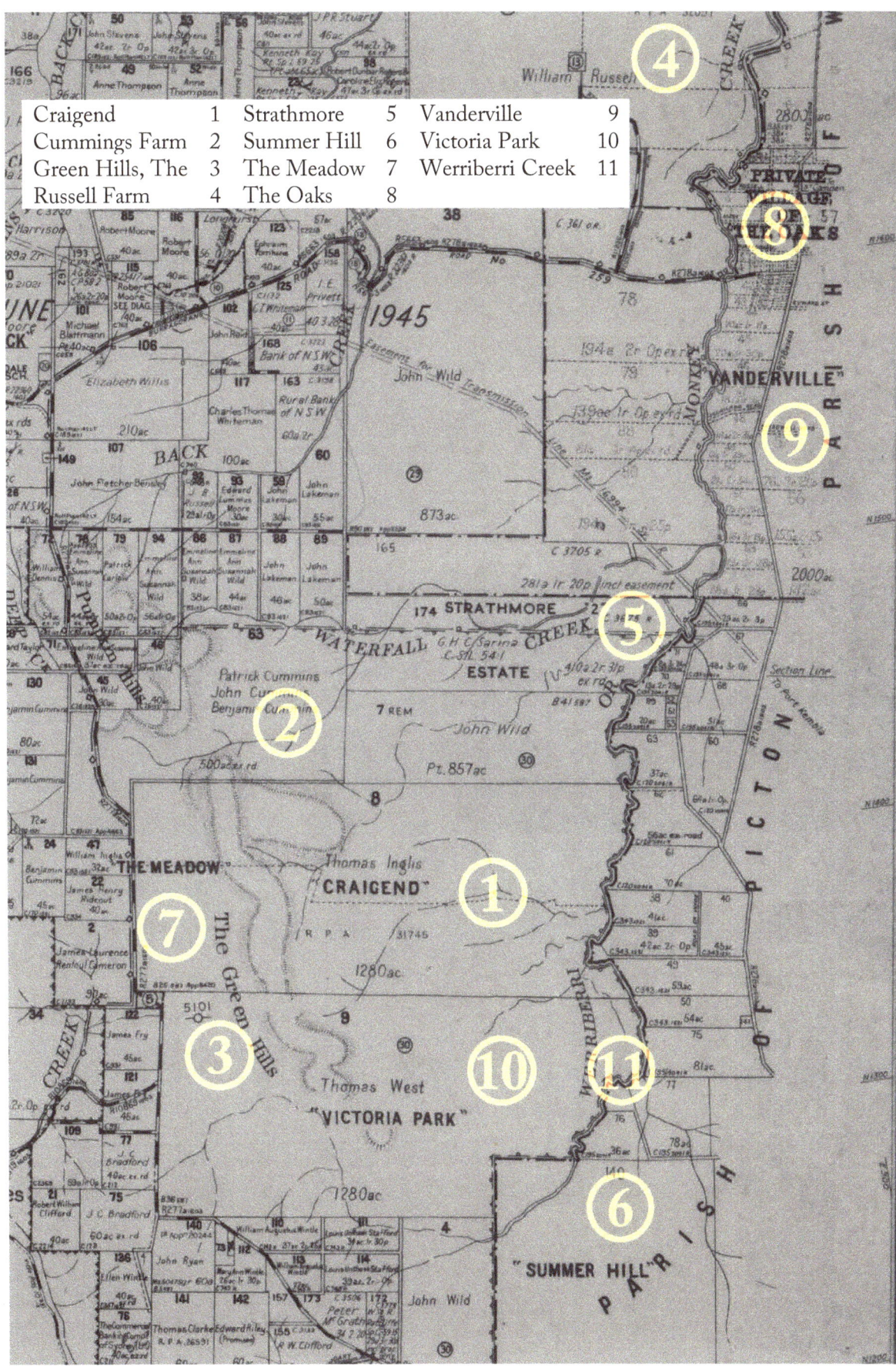

Parish Map Locations

MAP 4 Parish of Picton

Brisbane Farm	1	Milton	8
Cawdor	2	Montpellier	9
Coldenham	3	Peach Tree Bend	10
Craigend	4	Vanderville	11
Daisy Vale	5	Victoria Park	12
Hermitage	6	Williamswood	13
Howey Farm	7		

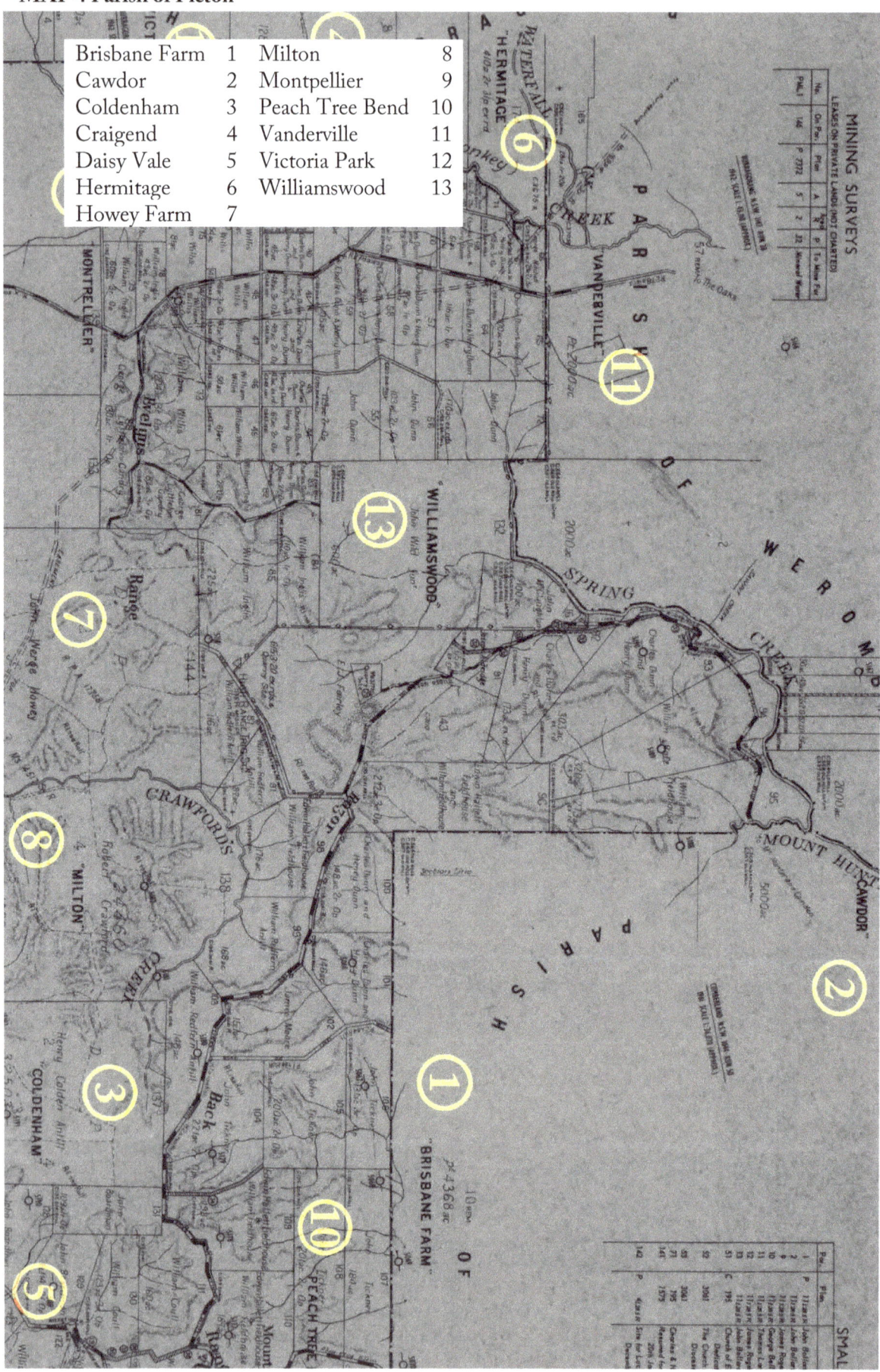

MAP 5 Parish of Picton

Abbotsford	1	Montpellier	8	Woodburn - Picton	15
Apperl	2	Seabright Park	9		
Coldenham	3	Stargard	10		
Fairy Hill	4	Stilton	11		
Howey Farm	5	Summer Hill	12		
Jarvisfield	6	Victoria Park	13		
Milton	7	Wellington Park	14		

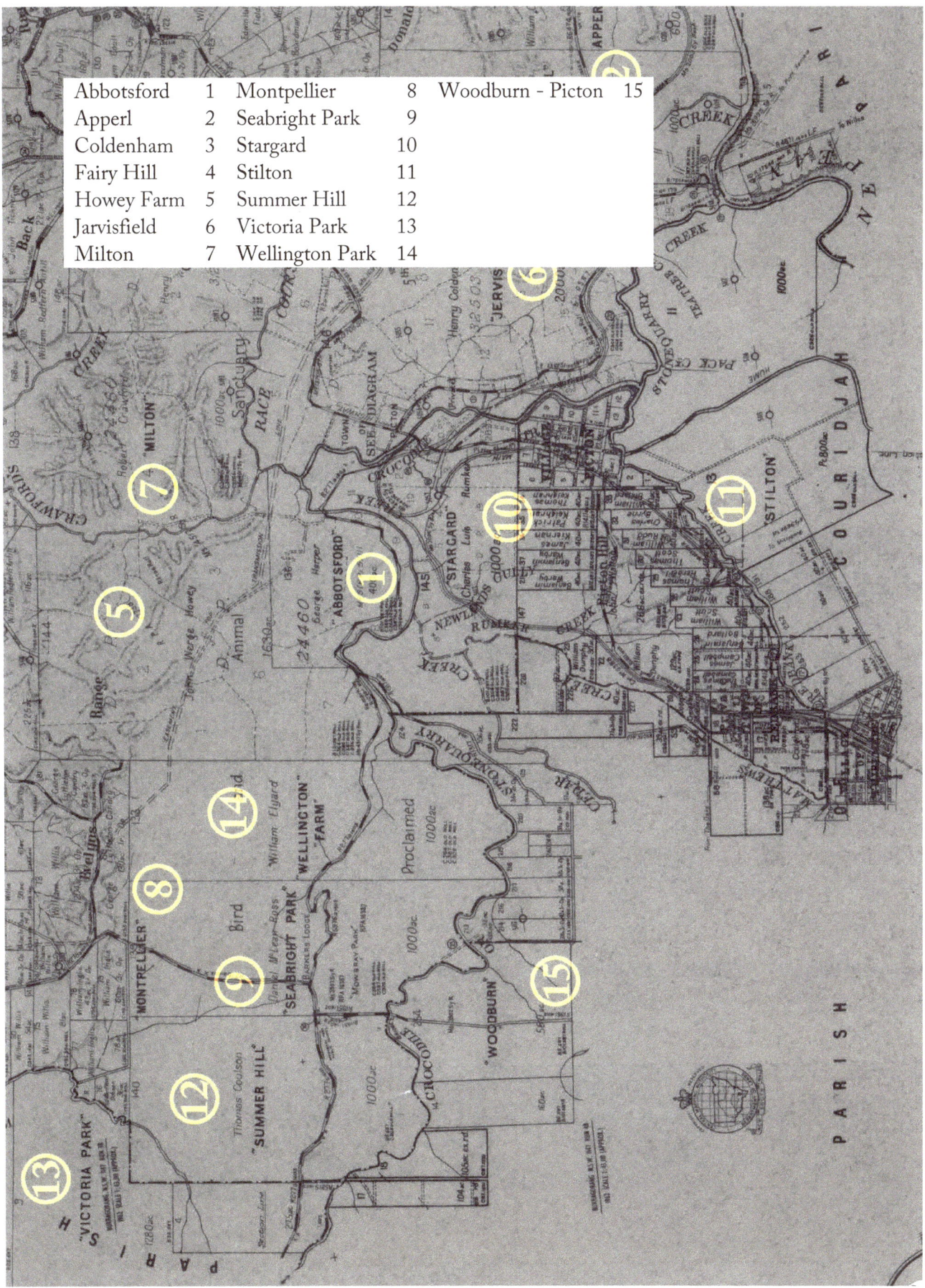

Parish Map Locations

MAP 6 Parish of Picton

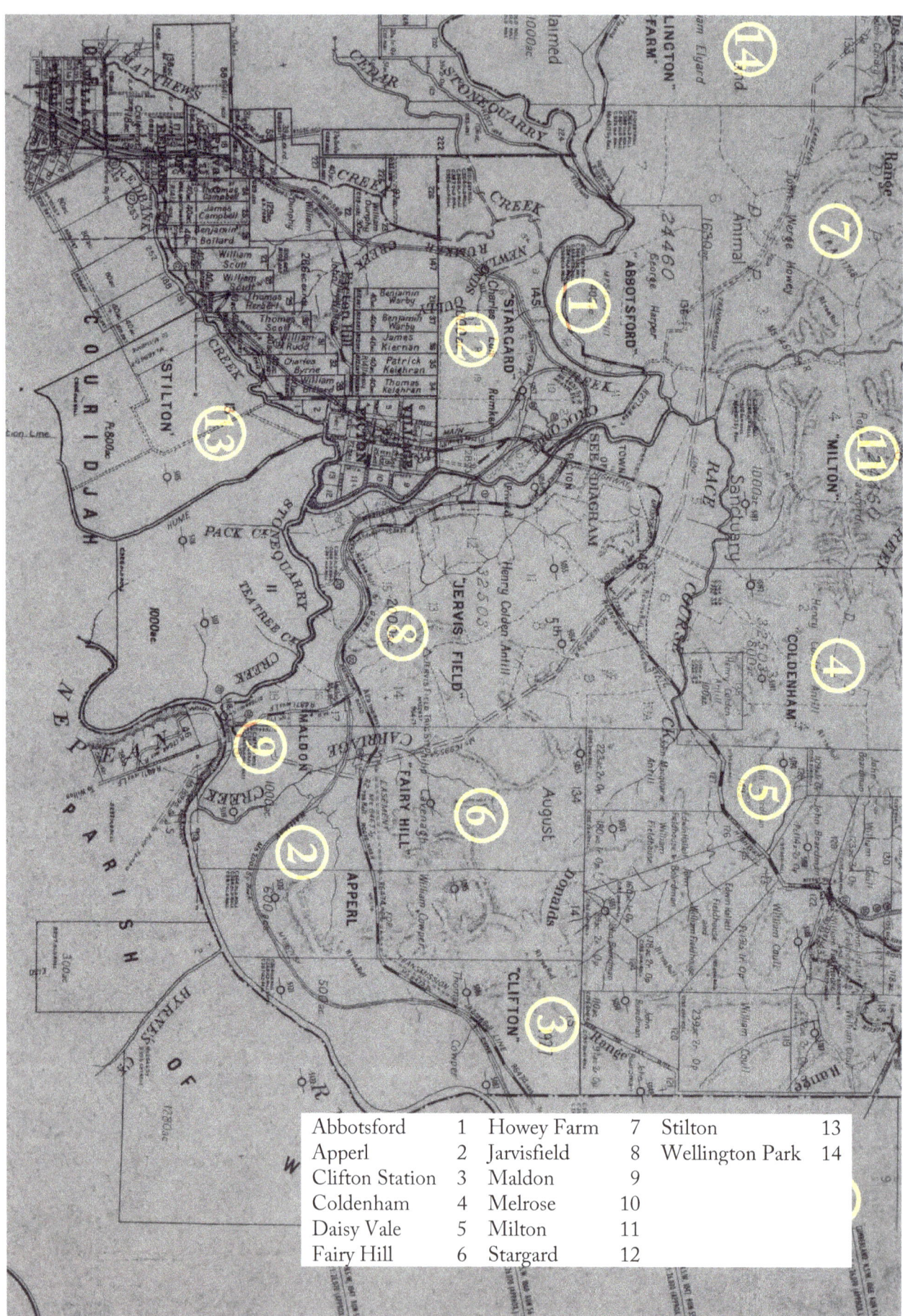

Abbotsford	1	Howey Farm	7	Stilton	13
Apperl	2	Jarvisfield	8	Wellington Park	14
Clifton Station	3	Maldon	9		
Coldenham	4	Melrose	10		
Daisy Vale	5	Milton	11		
Fairy Hill	6	Stargard	12		

Parish Map Locations

MAP 7 Parish of Camden

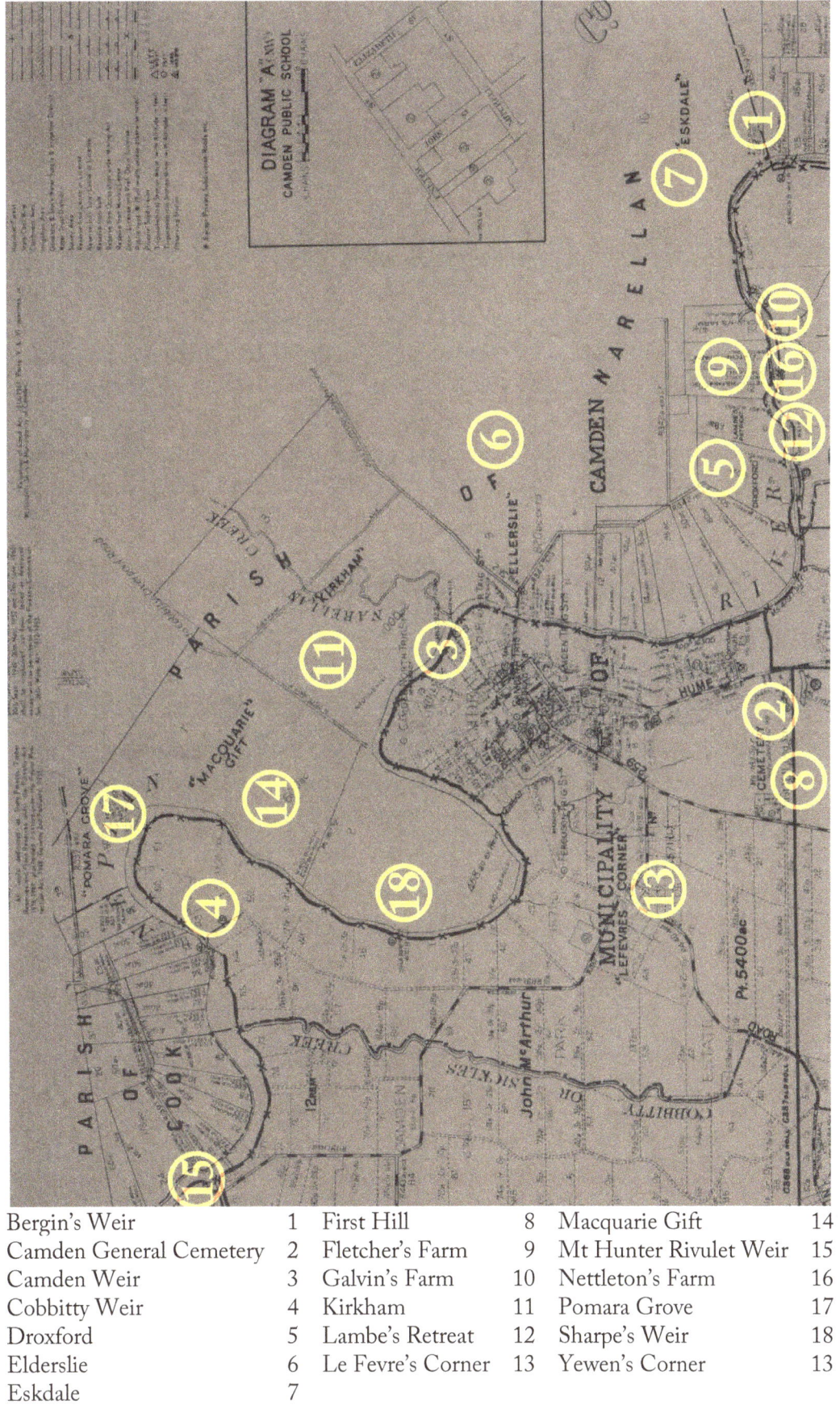

Bergin's Weir		1	First Hill	8	Macquarie Gift	14
Camden General Cemetery	2	Fletcher's Farm	9	Mt Hunter Rivulet Weir	15
Camden Weir		3	Galvin's Farm	10	Nettleton's Farm	16
Cobbitty Weir		4	Kirkham	11	Pomara Grove	17
Droxford		5	Lambe's Retreat	12	Sharpe's Weir	18
Elderslie		6	Le Fevre's Corner	13	Yewen's Corner	13
Eskdale		7				

83

Parish Map Locations

MAP 8 Parish of Cook - map dated 8 January 1885

Ballymacammon	1
Bents Basin	2
Bringelly	3
Brownlow Hill	4
Cobbitty	5
Cobbitty Trig	6
Cubbady	7
Cut Hill	8
Denbigh	9
Greendale	10

Hill Paddock	11
Kenmere	12
McArthur Flats	13
Newstead	14
Shankamore	15
Speed Farm	16
Vermont	17
Westwood	18
Wolverton	19

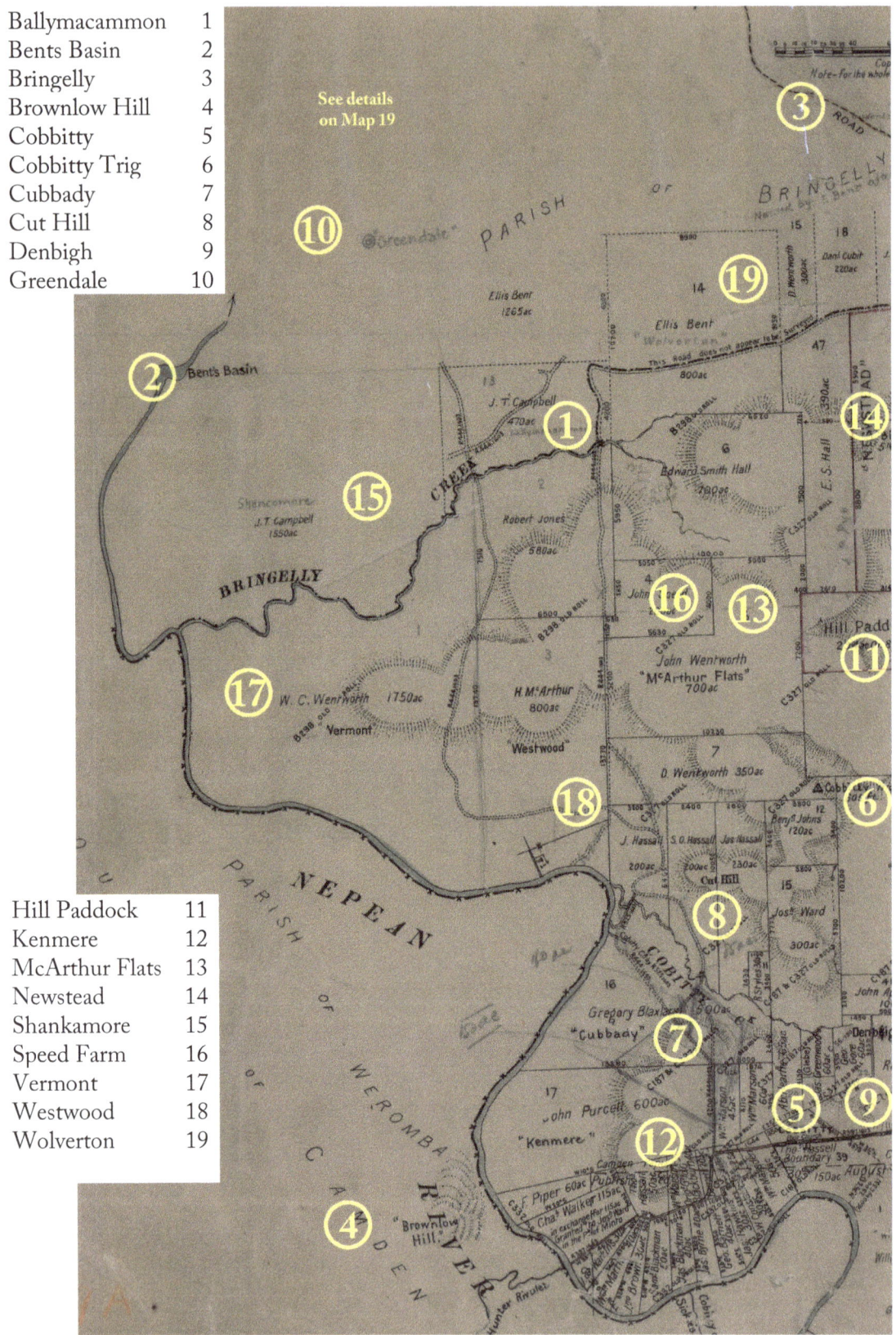

Parish Map Locations

MAP 9 Parish of Cook – map dated 8 January 1885

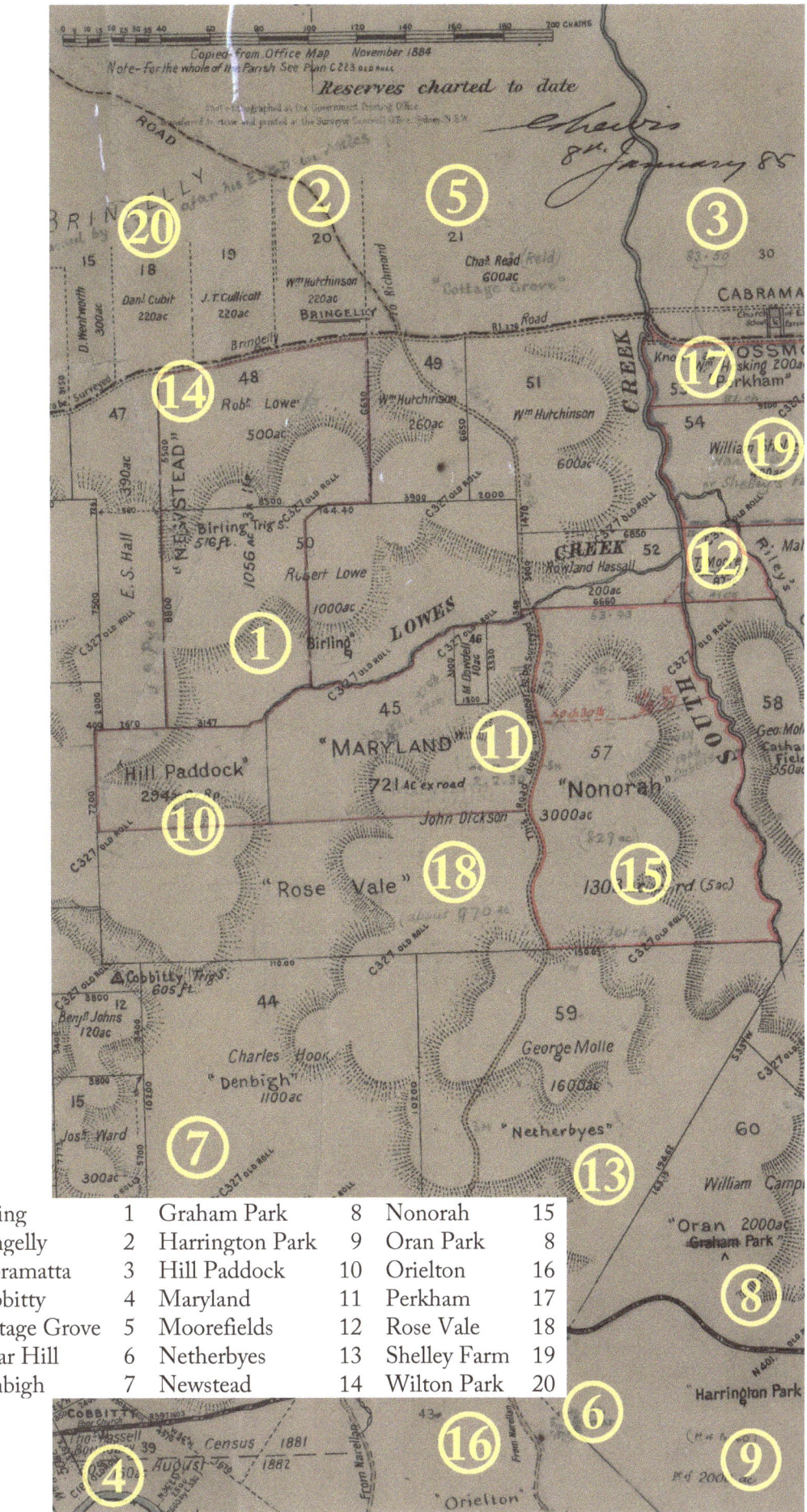

Birling	1	Graham Park	8	Nonorah	15
Bringelly	2	Harrington Park	9	Oran Park	8
Cabramatta	3	Hill Paddock	10	Orielton	16
Cobbitty	4	Maryland	11	Perkham	17
Cottage Grove	5	Moorefields	12	Rose Vale	18
Crear Hill	6	Netherbyes	13	Shelley Farm	19
Denbigh	7	Newstead	14	Wilton Park	20

Parish Map Locations

MAP 10 Parish of Cook – map dated 8 January 1885

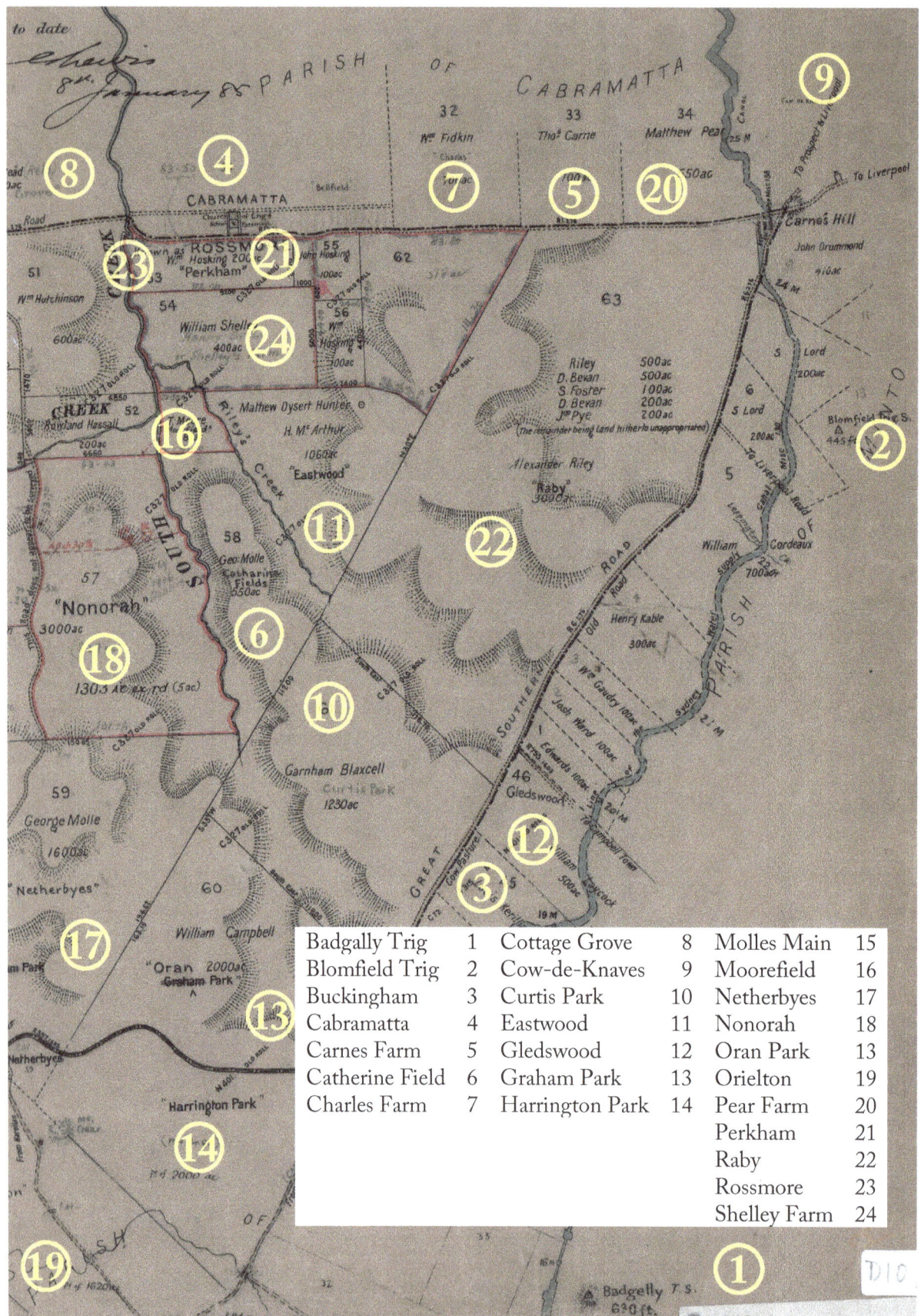

Badgally Trig	1	Cottage Grove	8	Molles Main	15
Blomfield Trig	2	Cow-de-Knaves	9	Moorefield	16
Buckingham	3	Curtis Park	10	Netherbyes	17
Cabramatta	4	Eastwood	11	Nonorah	18
Carnes Farm	5	Gledswood	12	Oran Park	13
Catherine Field	6	Graham Park	13	Orielton	19
Charles Farm	7	Harrington Park	14	Pear Farm	20
				Perkham	21
				Raby	22
				Rossmore	23
				Shelley Farm	24

Parish Map Locations

MAP 11 Parish of Cook – map dated 31 July 1928

Cabramatta	1	Cow-de-Knaves	4
Cottage Grove	2	Lucas Farm	5
Cottage Vale	3	Rossmore School	6

Parish Map Locations

MAP 12 Parish of Cook - map dated 31 July 1928

Ballymacammon	1	Cottage Grove	4	Wilton Park	7
Bathurst Farm	2	Cottage Vale	5	Wolverton	8
Campbell Park	3	Lucas Farm	6		

Parish Map Locations

MAP 13 Parish of Cook - map dated 31 July 1928

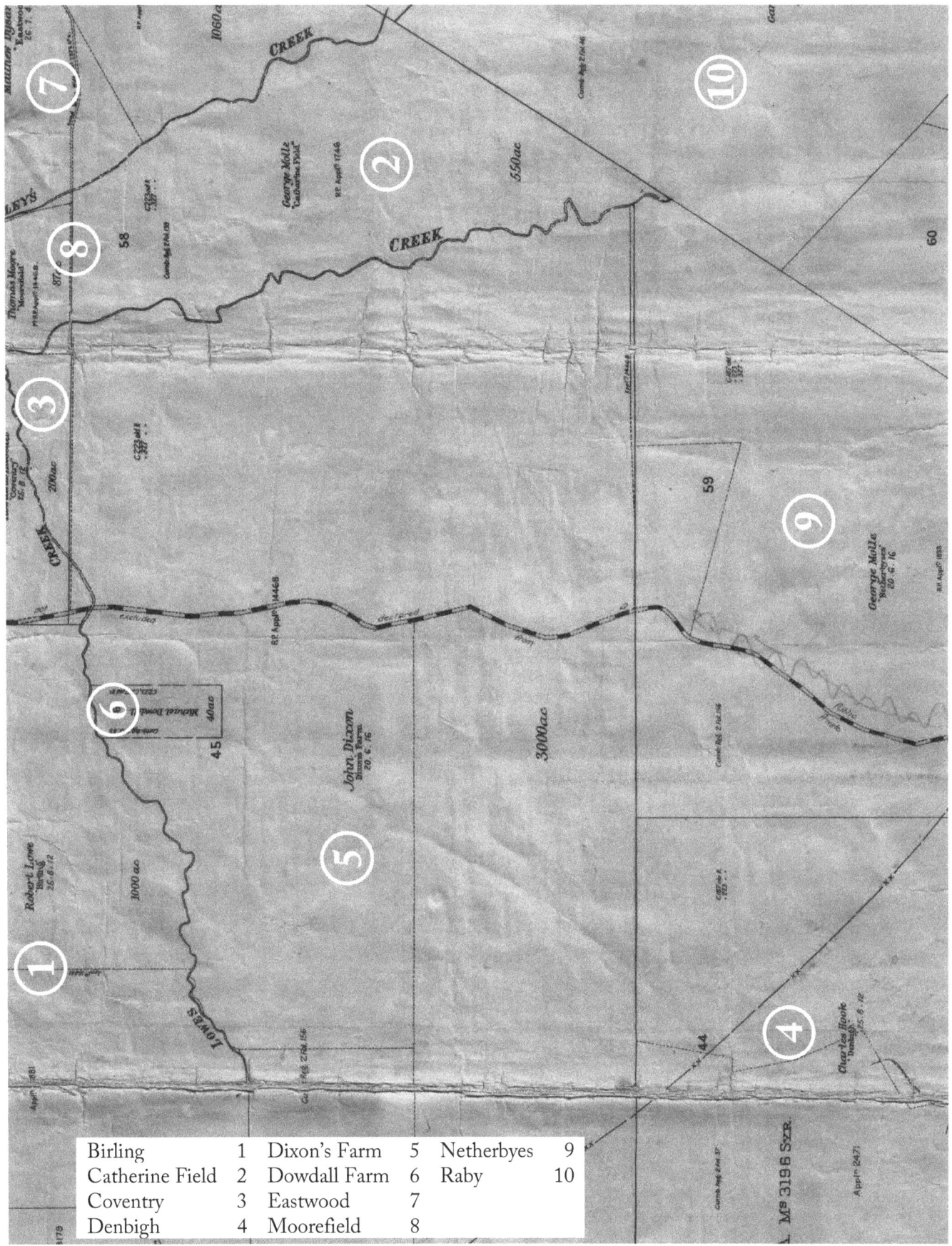

Birling	1	Dixon's Farm	5	Netherbyes	9
Catherine Field	2	Dowdall Farm	6	Raby	10
Coventry	3	Eastwood	7		
Denbigh	4	Moorefield	8		

Parish Map Locations

MAP 14 Parish of Cook - map dated 31 July 1928

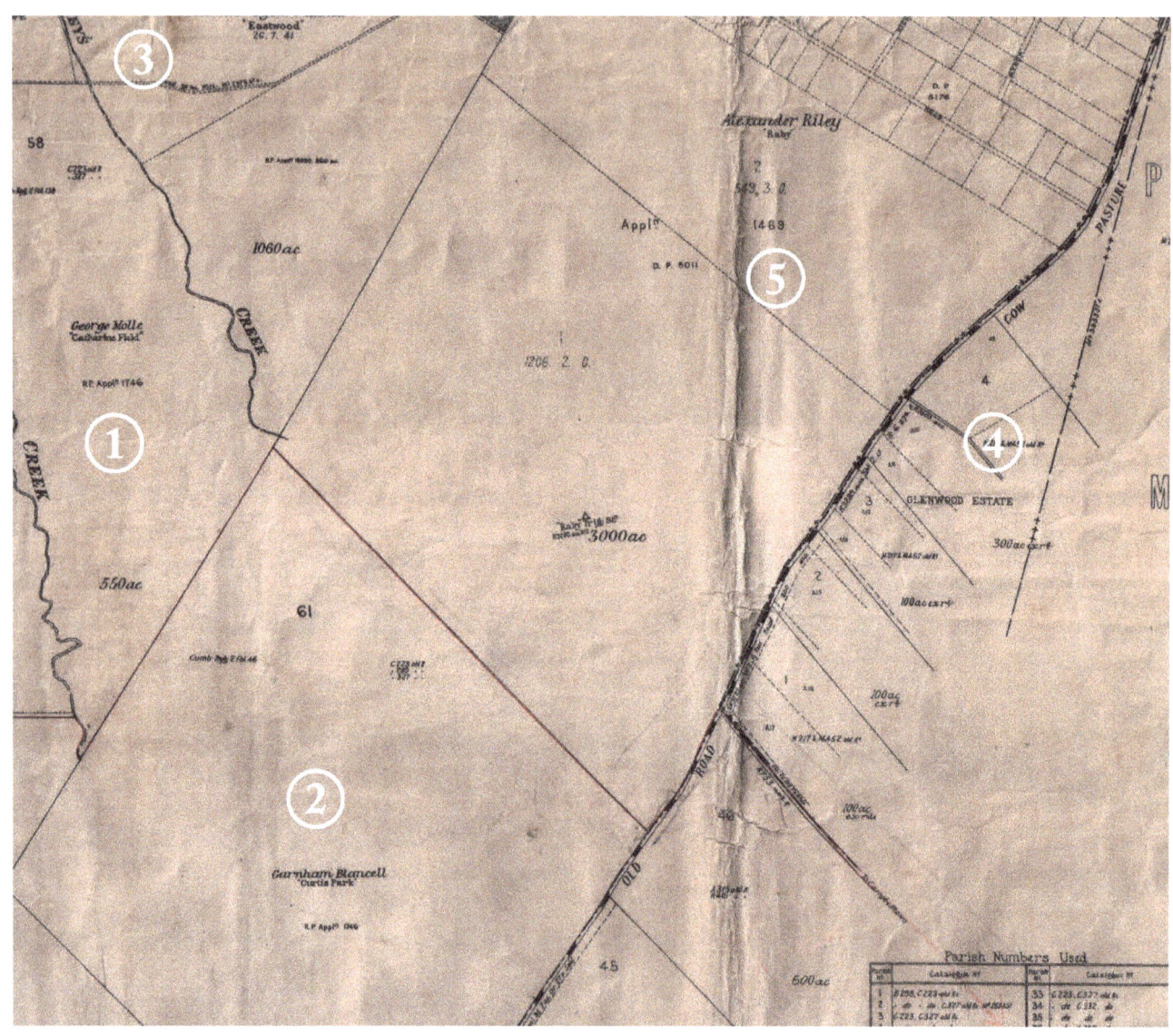

Catherine Field 1   Eastwood   3   Raby   5
Curtis Park   2   Gledswood 4

MAP 15 Parish of Cook - map dated 31 July 1928

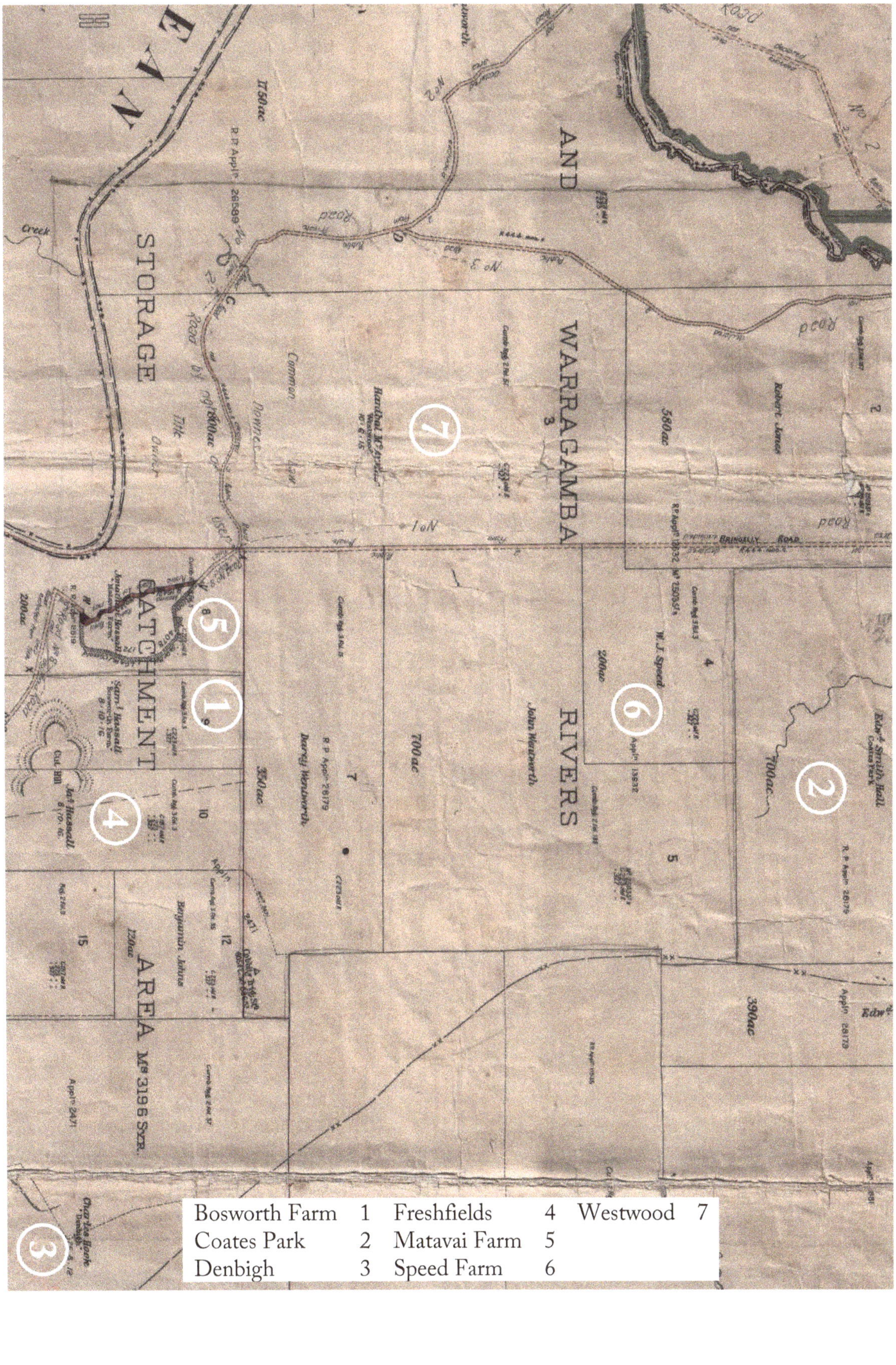

Bosworth Farm	1	Freshfields	4	Westwood	7
Coates Park	2	Matavai Farm	5		
Denbigh	3	Speed Farm	6		

Parish Map Locations

MAP 16 Parish of Cook - map dated 31 July 1928

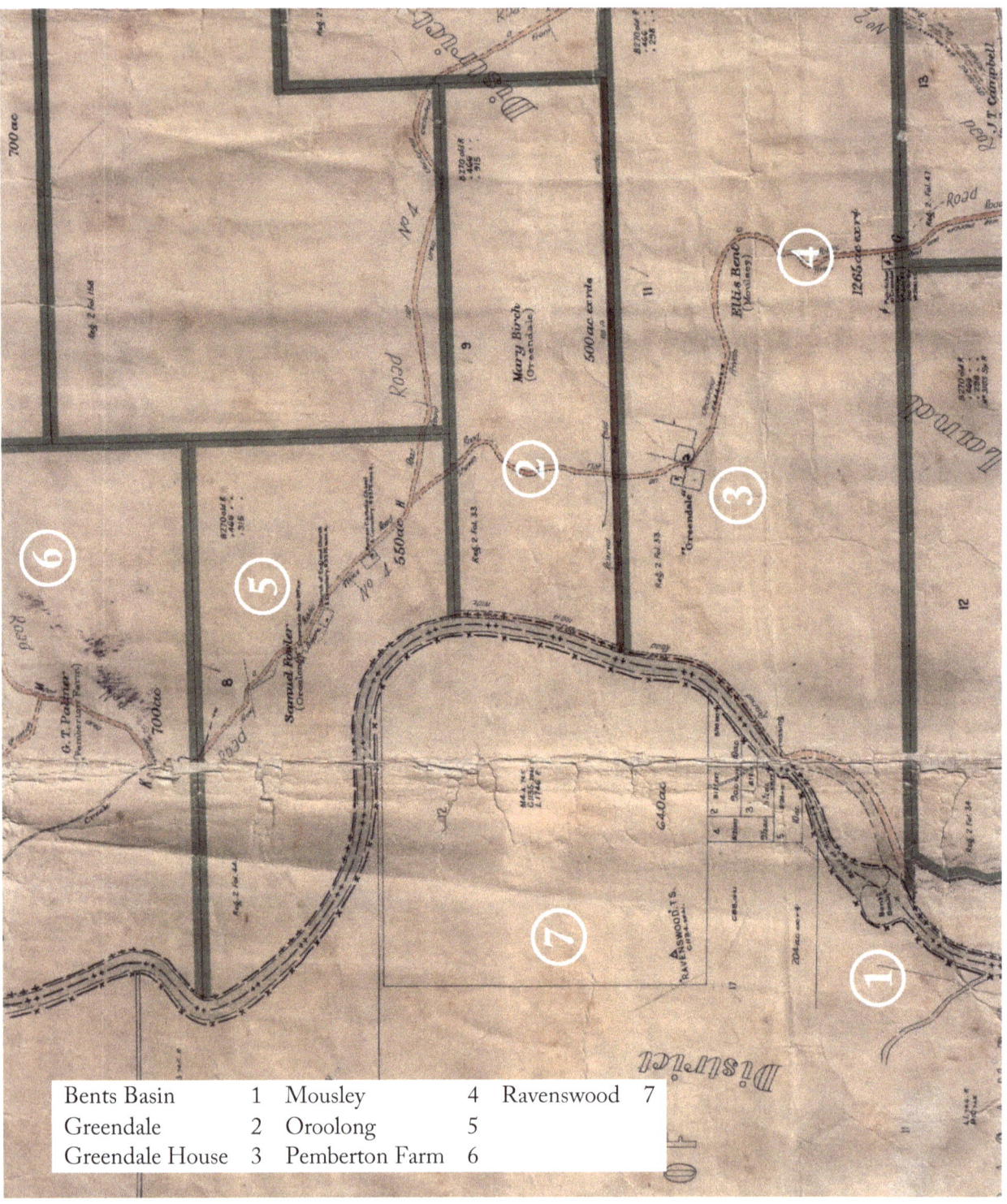

Bents Basin	1	Mousley	4	Ravenswood	7
Greendale	2	Oroolong	5		
Greendale House	3	Pemberton Farm	6		

Parish Map Locations

MAP 17 Parish of Camden

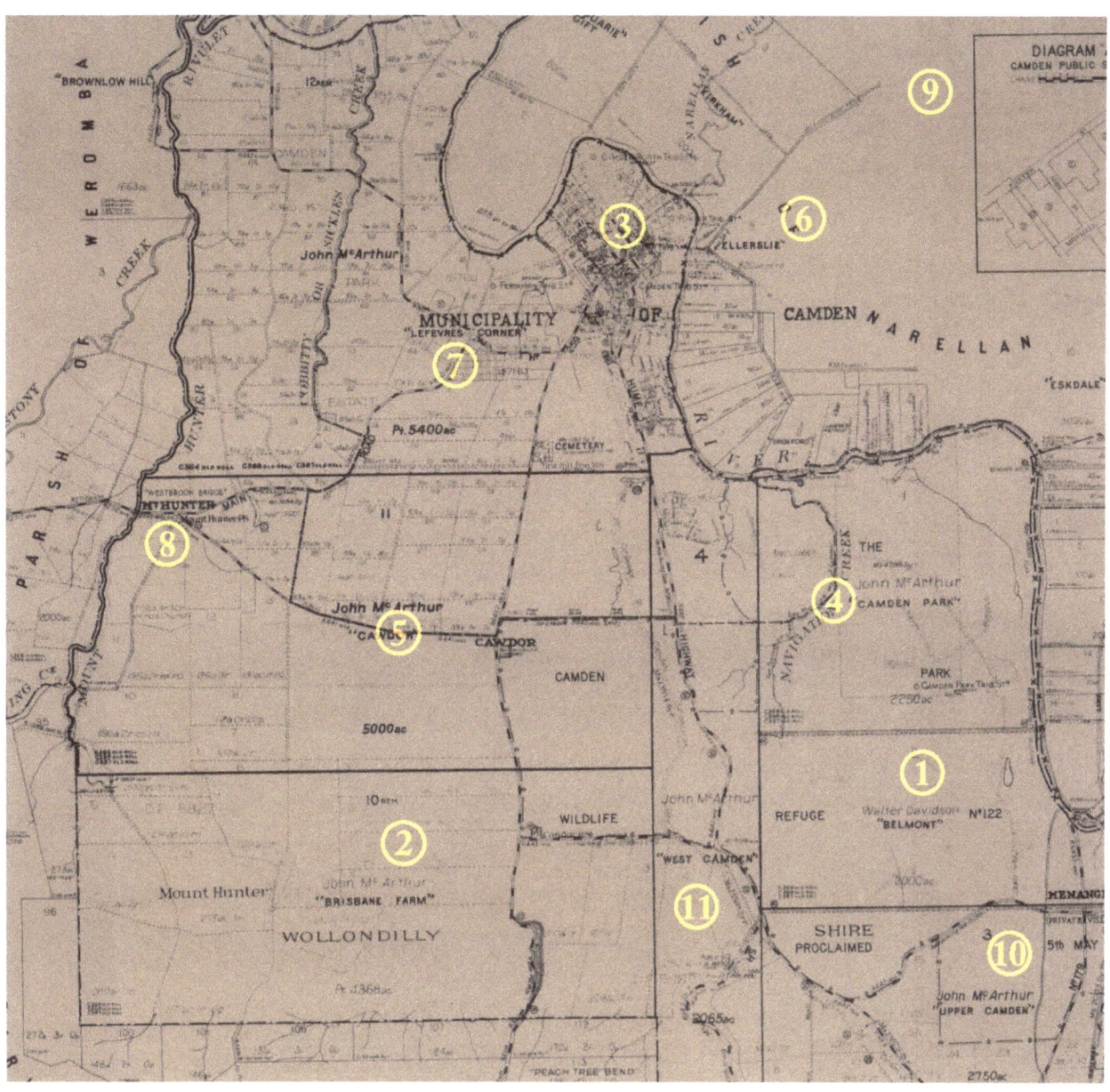

Belmont	1	Elderslie	6	West Camden	11
Brisbane Farm	2	Le Fevre's Corner	7		
Camden	3	Mount Hunter	8		
Camden Park	4	Narellan	9		
Cawdor	5	Upper Camden	10		

Parish Map Locations

MAP 18 Parish of Camden

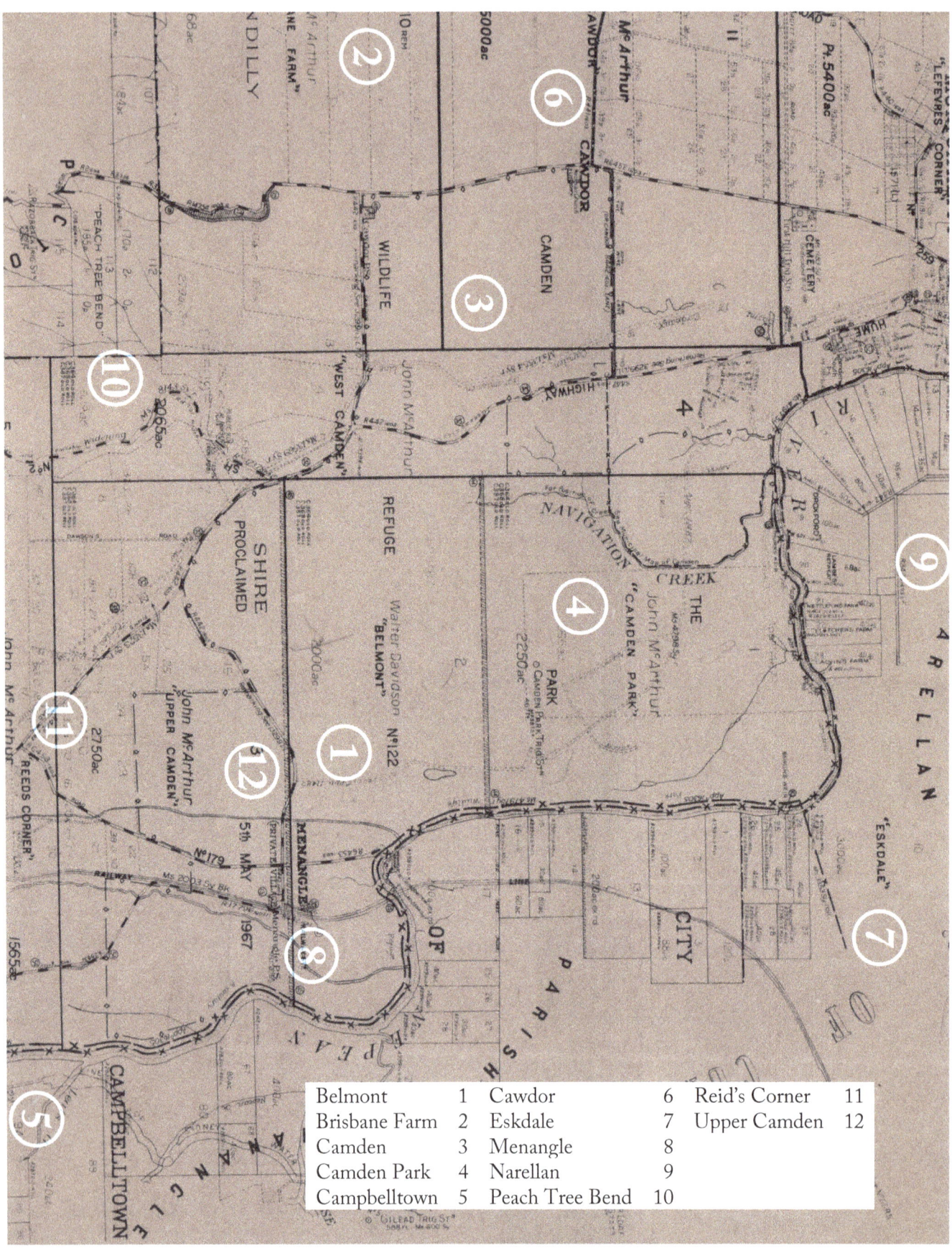

Belmont	1	Cawdor	6	Reid's Corner	11
Brisbane Farm	2	Eskdale	7	Upper Camden	12
Camden	3	Menangle	8		
Camden Park	4	Narellan	9		
Campbelltown	5	Peach Tree Bend	10		

MAP 19 Parish of Camden

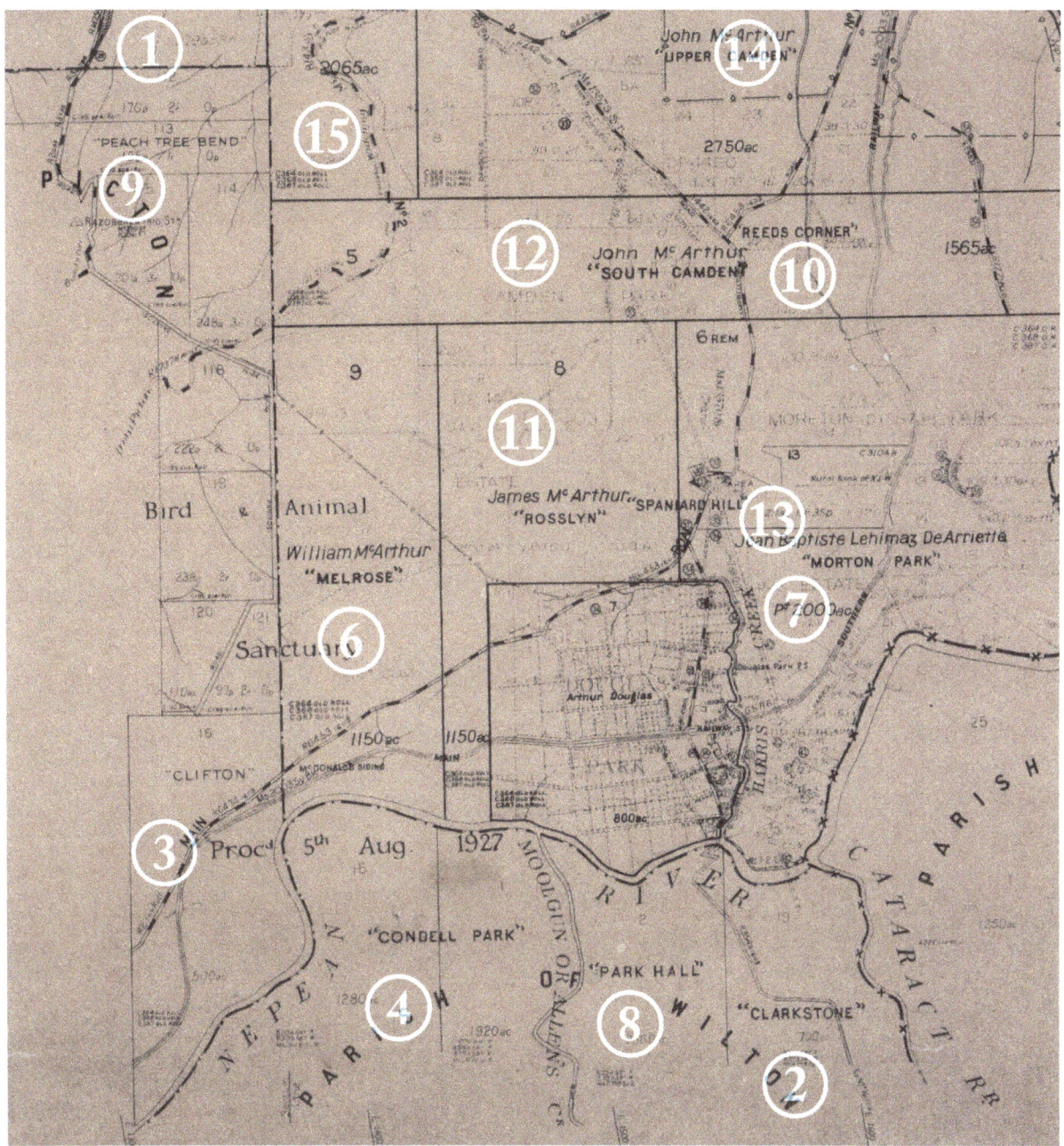

Brisbane Farm	1	Moreton Park	7	Spaniard's Hill	13
Clarkstone	2	Park Hall	8	Upper Camden	14
Clifton	3	Peach Tree Bend	9	West Camden	15
Condell Park	4	Reid's Corner	10		
Douglas Park	5	Rosslyn	11		
Melrose	6	South Camden	12		

The Township of Camden 1850s

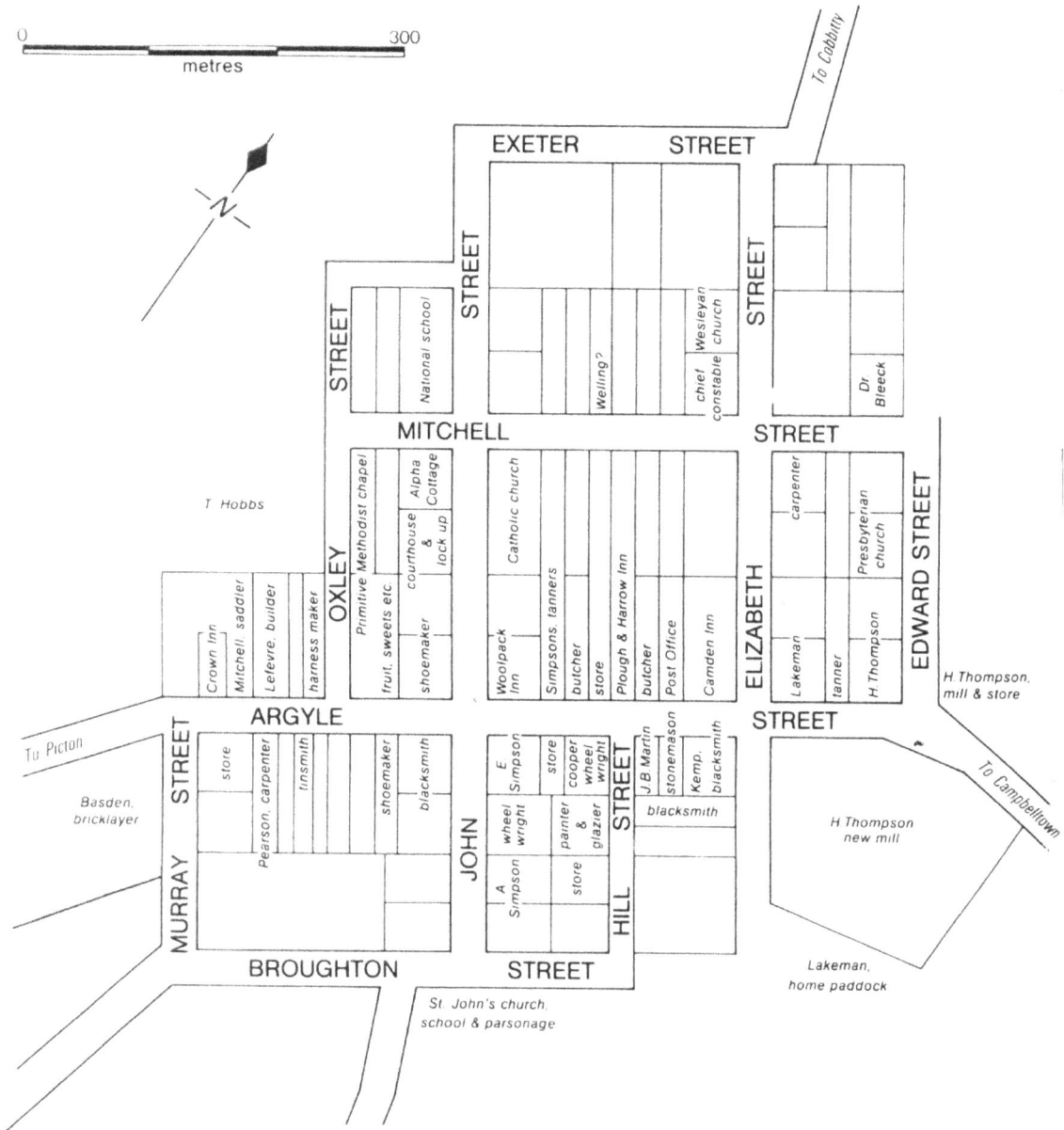

Plan of the Town of Camden - photo courtesy of Alan Atkinson: Camden, Farm and Village Life in Early New South Wales

Camden Park Estate Sales

In 1887 Thomas Dawson oversaw the sale of the North Cawdor Estate on instructions from the Camden Park Estate. There were both large and small farm lots, including Mount Hunter, Grasmere, and land along Macquarie Grove Road. Prospective purchases were given an attractive booklet indicating lots already sold and still available. Those already leasing the land from the Camden Park Estate took many of the lots.

Reproduction of these maps and others follow, along with known landowners.

All maps can be accessed through the Camden Museum, and the booklet mentioned can be viewed.

Index to Lots - Maps 20 - 26

Name		Lots	Map
Armitage	Section 11	8 & 9	22
Axam, Joseph	Cawdor	38	24
Bank of NSW	Town	Section 7	20
Baxter, James	Cawdor	19	24
Bennett, Alfred	Cawdor	33, 36, 66-67 & 90-93	24
Blackman, George Albert	Section 12	5	23
Bourke, William Joseph	Section 12	16 & 17	23
Bugden, Elizabeth	Section 11	14	22
Bugden, Henry	Cawdor	94	24
Camden Rail Terminus	Town	Section 4	20
Camden Railway Station	Town	Section 8	20
Camden Town Hall	Town	Section 7	20
Carrington Hospital Estate	Section 11		22
Carter, John	Cawdor	9, 10 & 11	24
Childs, John William	Cawdor	37	24
Chisholm, Dr Edwin	Town	Section 1	20
Clarke, James	Cawdor	24 & 25	24
Cliff, John W	Cawdor	16 & 17	24
Clifton, Henry Sivyer	Cawdor	75	24
Clout, Edward Michael	Cawdor	20, 26 & 27	24
Commercial Bank	Town	Section 6	20
Cottage Hospital	Section 12	1	23
Crick, William	Section 12	14	23
Crown Hotel	Town	Section 5	20
Curry	Cawdor	88	24
Davies, Evan Alfred	Cawdor	5. 6, 7	24
Doust, David	Cawdor	21, 22, 23	24
Dowle, Charles William	Section 12	25	23
Fenning, George	Cawdor	49 & 53	24
Ferguson, Francis	Cawdor		24
Fryer, John	Cawdor	55. 56 & 71-74	24
Fuller, George	Cawdor	69	24
Funnell, Thomas	Section 13	9	21
Furner, Walter Charles	Section 11	18	22
Furner, Walter Charles	Section 12	6, 7, 12 & 13	23
Griffiths, Edward George	Cawdor	18	24
Head, H	Cawdor	5 - 7	24
Huntley, William James	Section 11	4	22
Huntley, William James	Section 12	24	23
Jackson, Dr William Hardy	Town	Section 1	20
Johnson, John	Cawdor	63	24
Johnson, Sarah Susan née Tavener	Cawdor	65	24
Kelloway, George William	Cawdor	86 & 87	24
Kelloway, John Thomas	Cawdor	85	24
Kelloway, John Thomas	Section 12	2	23
Larkin, Willie	Section 13	15	21

Name		Lots	Map
Maher, John	Cawdor	35 & 39	24
Marshall, R	Cawdor	68, 89	24
May, Percy Withers	Section 11	1	22
McCulloch, Alexander	Cawdor	48	24
Miller, James Lovell	Cawdor	44	24
Moore, Henry (dec'd)	Section 13	8	21
Moore, John Edward	Section 13	11, 12, 13, & 14	21
New, Charles Edward	Section 11	7	22
Onslow Park	Section 11		22
Paling, William Henry	Cawdor	12-13, 45-47, & 62	24
Peat, John	Section 13	6	21
Peters, Walter Frederick	Section 13	7	21
Pinkerton, James Frederick John	Section 12	9, 10 & 11	23
Plough & Harrow Hotel	Town	Section 7	20
Police Court	Town	Section 6	20
Poole, Frank Elias George	Section 12	15	23
Poole, John William	Section 11	5 & 6	22
Porter, George Alexander	Cawdor	79 - 83	24
Post Office	Town	Section 6	20
Public School	Town		20
Rapley, Eliza Jane	Section 11	3	22
Reeves, Henry Pollock	Town	Section 3	20
Roman Catholic Church	Town	Section 7	20
Roman Catholic Presbytery	Town	Section 3	20
Rootes, James	Cawdor	60	24
Royal Hotel	Town	Section 7	20
Salter, James Albert	Section 11	11, 12 & 13	22
Sheather, James	Cawdor	42	24
Simpson, Ebeneezer	Cawdor	70	24
Simpson, Ebeneezer Jr	Town	Section 2	20
Sloan, Peter	Cawdor		26
Smith, Charles Philip	Section 12	3 & 4	23
Smith, Thomas	Cawdor	84	24
Smith, William	Cawdor	61	24
Spice, Henry	Cawdor	40	24
St John's Church	Town		20
Stimson, William	Cawdor	43	24
Stuckey, Walter	Section 11	16	22
Taplin, Alfred Edwin	Section 13	2	21
Taplin, William John	Section 13	10	21
Telegraph Office	Town	Section 7	20
Thompson, Charles Augustus	Cawdor	30	24
Thorn, Charles	Cawdor	51, 52 & 57	24
Tritton, Alfred John	Section 12	18 & 19	23
Walsh, Eustace Henry	Section 13	1	21
Wasson, James	Section 11	10	22
Waterworth Hotel	Section 11		22
Wheeler, Edmund	Cawdor	95 & 96	24

Camden Park Estate Sales

Name	Lots		Map
Wheeler, James	Cawdor		26
Whiteman, Charles Thomas	Cawdor	58 & 59	24
Whiteman, Charles Thomas	Section 11	2, 15 & 19-21	22
Whiteman, Charles Thomas	Section 12	28	23
Wilkinson, William	Section 12	20, 21. 22. 23, 26 & 27	23
Wilkinson, William	Section 13	3, 4 & 5	21

MAP 20 Land Sales Town – map dated 13 March 1898

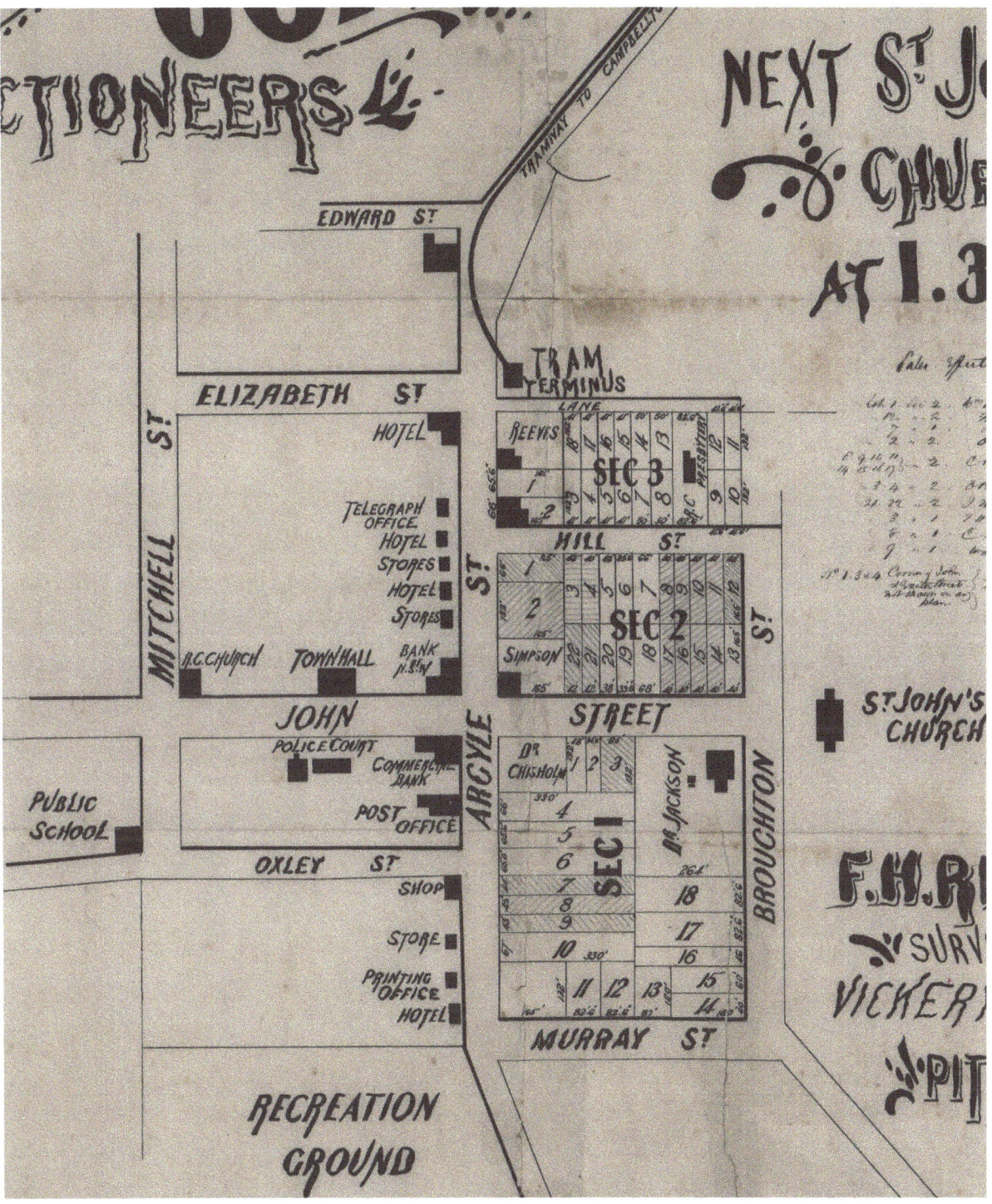

Camden Park Estate Sales

MAP 21 Land Sales Section 13 – map c.1900

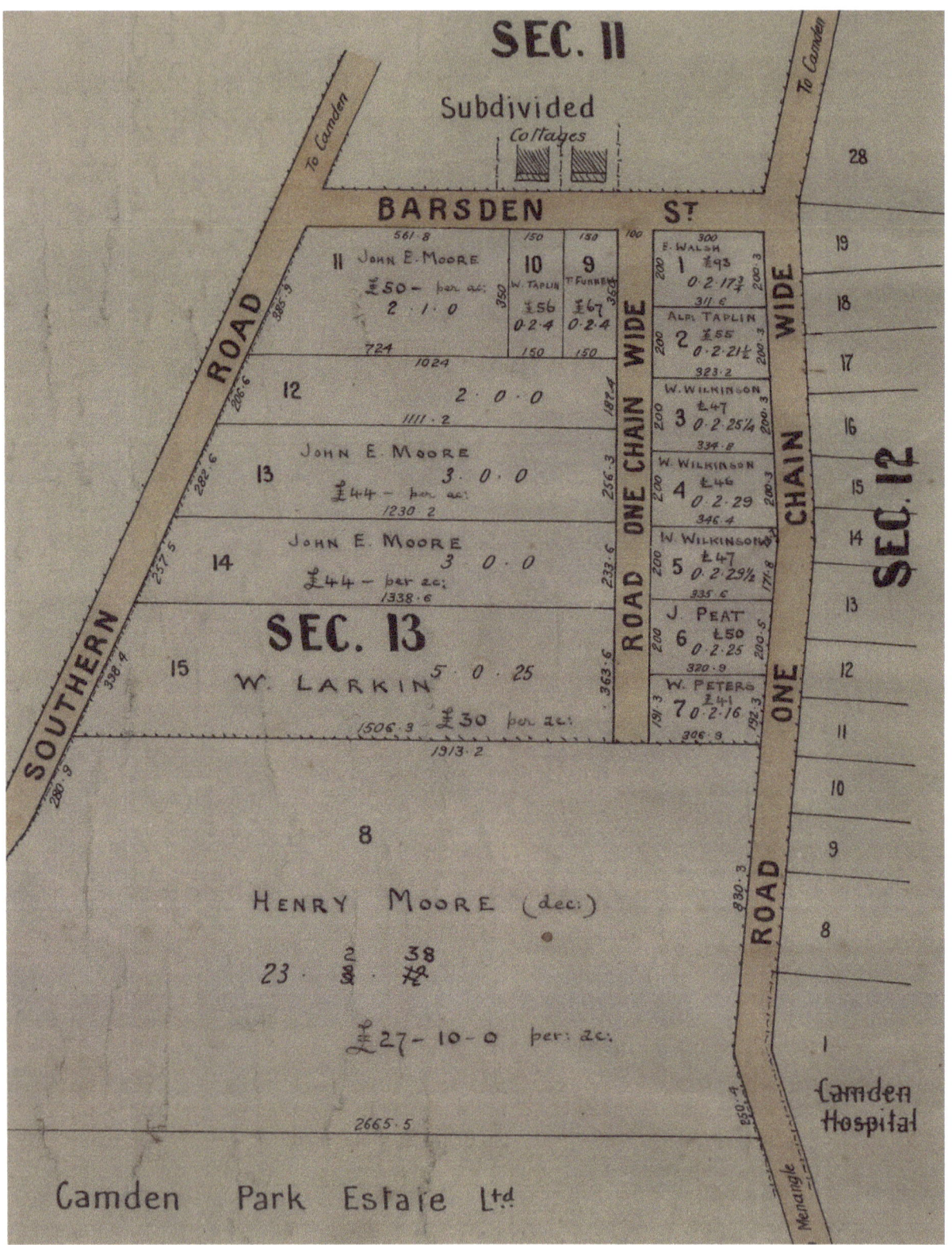

MAP 22 Land Sales Section 11 – map dated 29 March 1898

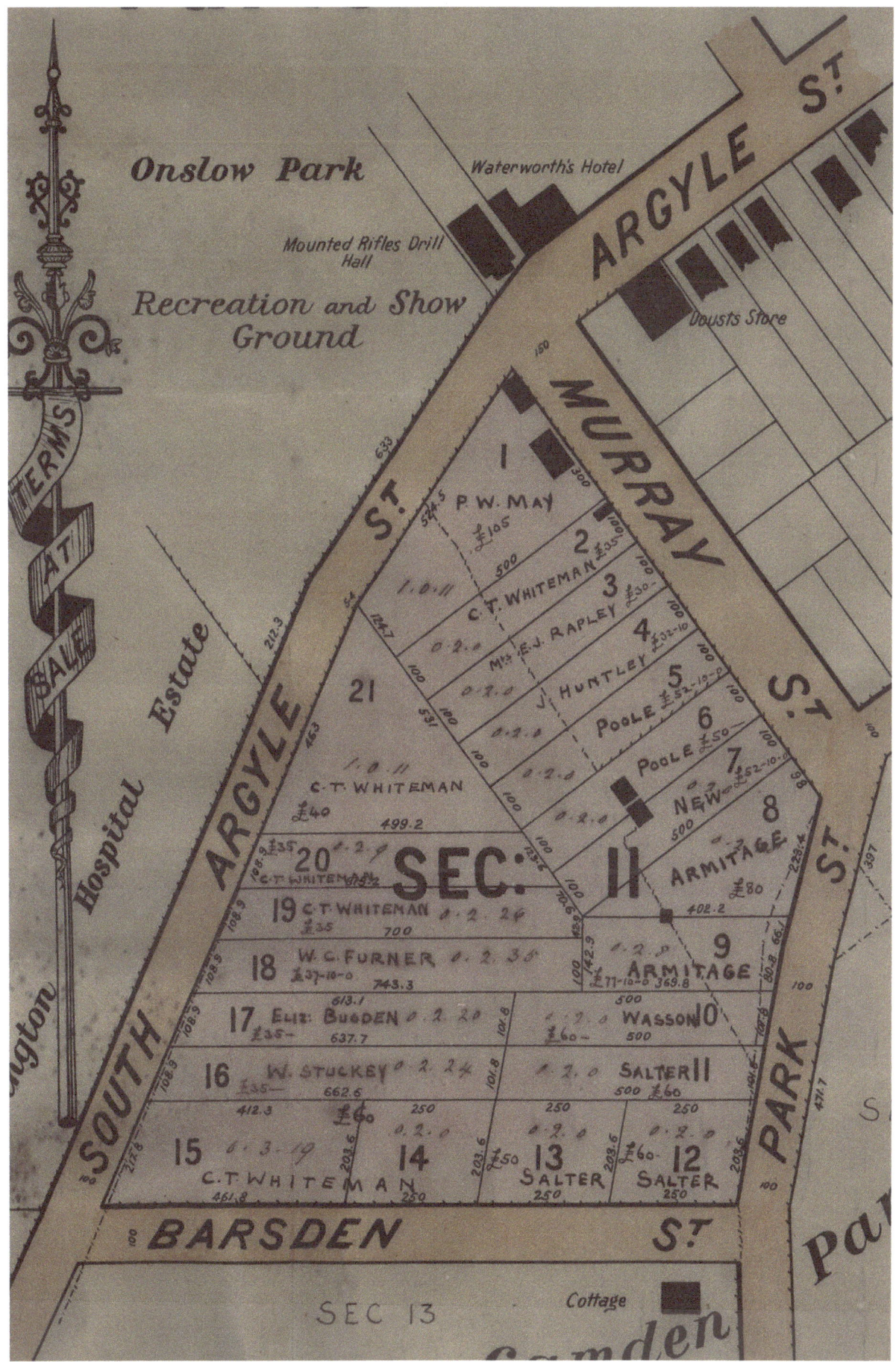

Camden Park Estate Sales

MAP 23 Land and Sales Section 12 – map dated 19 February 1900

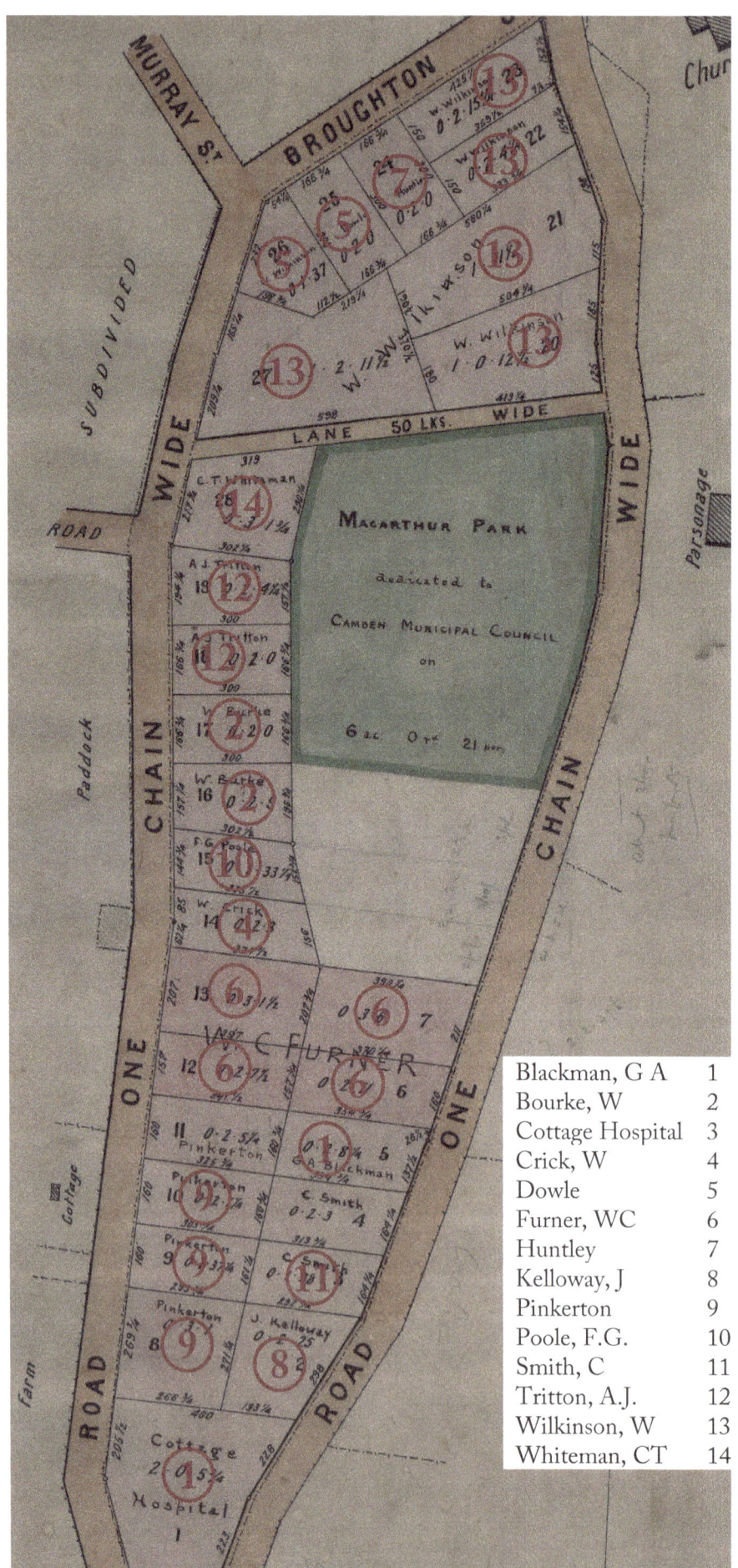

Name	No.
Blackman, G A	1
Bourke, W	2
Cottage Hospital	3
Crick, W	4
Dowle	5
Furner, WC	6
Huntley	7
Kelloway, J	8
Pinkerton	9
Poole, F.G.	10
Smith, C	11
Tritton, A.J.	12
Wilkinson, W	13
Whiteman, CT	14

MAP 24 Land Sales 1887 - North Cawdor Estate – Plan 1

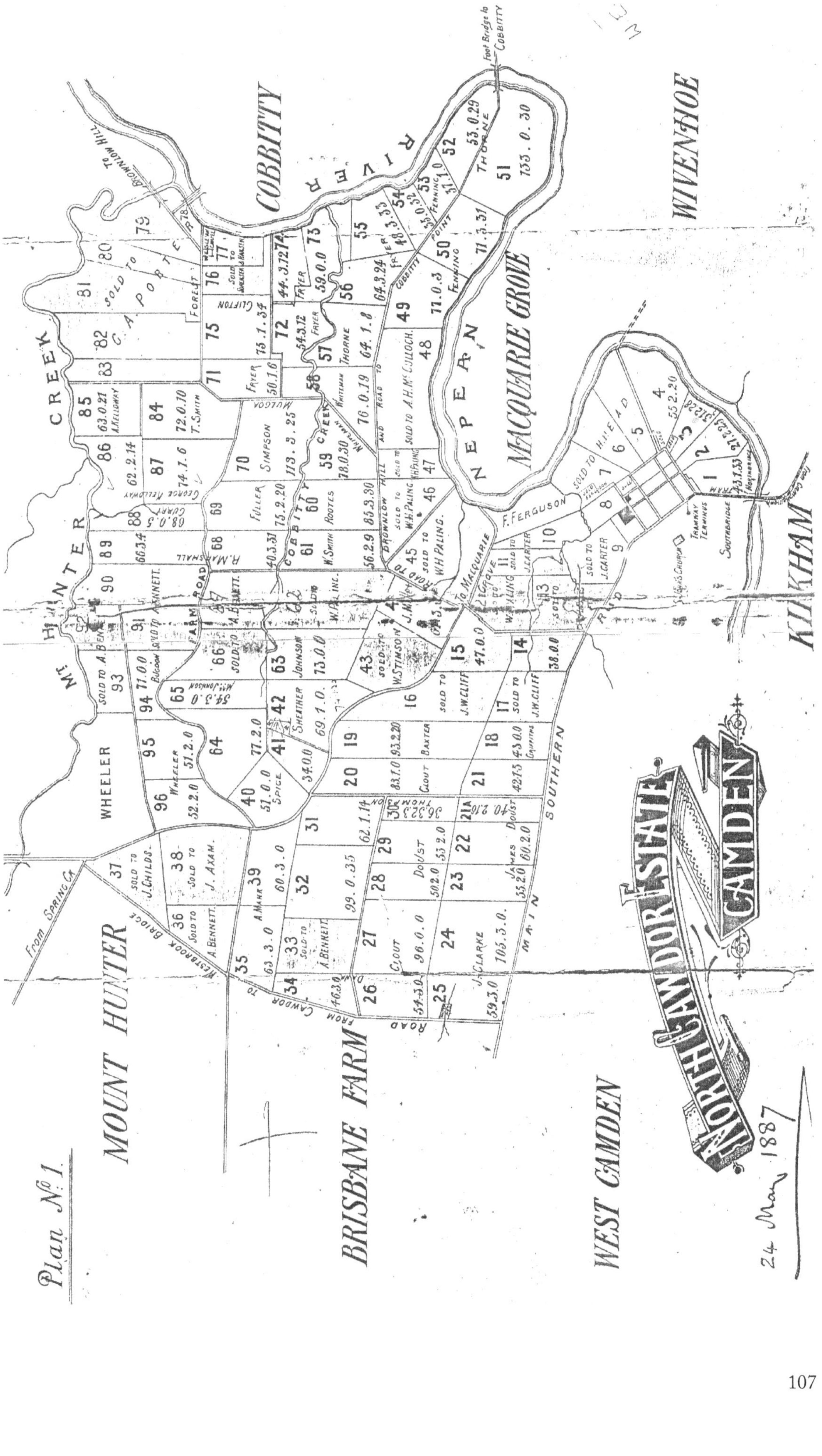

Camden Park Estate Sales

MAP 25 Land Sales 1887 - North Cawdor Estate – Plan 2

Camden Park Estate Sales

MAP 26 Land Sales 1887 -North Cawdor Estate – Plan 3

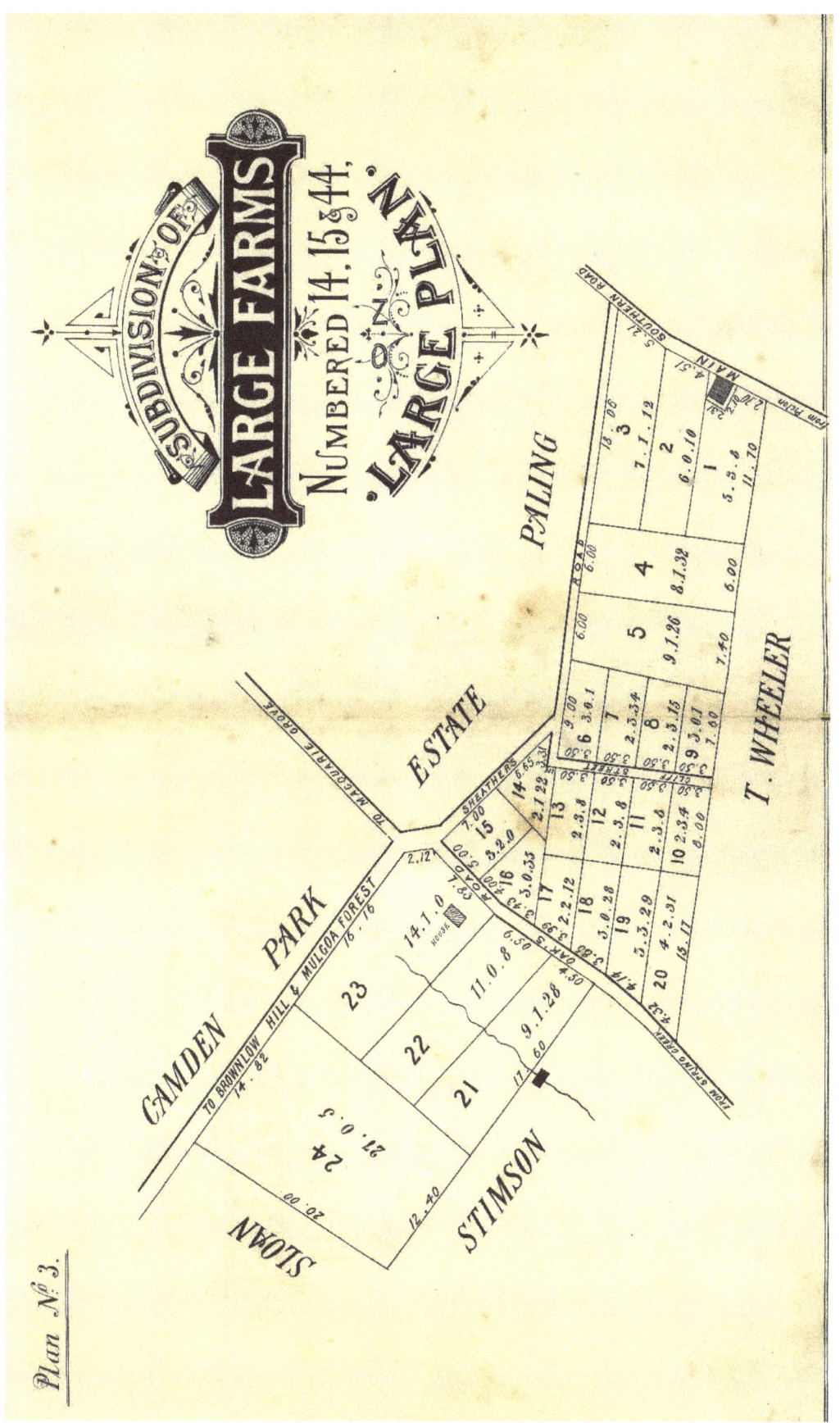

109

Bibliography

Atkinson, Alan: Camden: Farm and village life in early New South Wales - North Melbourne, Vic.: Australian Scholarly Publishing, 2008

Burnett, Brian, Johnson, Janice Johnson, Nixon, Richard, Wrigley, John: They worked at Camden Park: a listing of the employees, leaseholders and tenant farmers known to have worked on the Camden Park Estate

Camden Council: Camden Local Environmental Plan 2010

Google Maps – https://www.google.com.au/maps/

McNaught, Jean: Index to Certificates of Depasturing Licences. Licence to Depasture Crown Lands Beyond Location –Richmond-Tweed Regional Library, Goonellabah, 1997

McNaught, Jean: Land grants – Leases and Purchases 1792-1865 – Richmond-Tweed Regional Library, Goonellabah, 1998

Norwood, Edward W with research by Speer, Albert MBE: William Charker Otherwise Chalker (1774-1823): His History – Gymea 1997

NSW Department of Primary Industries: Reducing the Impact of Weirs on Aquatic Habitat, NSW Detailed Weir Review

Santy, Malcolm R and Johnson, Keith A: Census of New South Wales November 1828 –Library of Australian History – Sydney 1980

Water NSW: Weirs - http://www.waternsw.com.au/supply/Greater-Sydney/weirs

Water NSW: Water Sharing Rules Middle Nepean River Management Zones

Index to Landowners, Tenants, and Others

A

Adams
   Annie Linda, 28
   Sidney William, 30
   William, 28, 30
Ainsworth
   William Carus, 56
Amos
   Thomas Setrop, 36
Anderson
   Clarice Vivian, 3
   Clarice Vivian Faithfull, 3
   Frances Lillian, 3, 17
   William Hugh, 3, 16, 38
Anschau
   Johann (John), 3
Antill
   Major Henry Colden, 21, 37
Ardill
   George Edward, 41
Arlow
   Elizabeth, 72
Arnold
   Samuel, 53
Atkins
   Judge Advocate Richard, 25
Auld
   Annie Linda, 28
Axam
   Joseph, 100

B

Badgery
   Andrew, 28
Baigent
   Brian Charles, 4
Baker
   Florence June, 12
Bardwell
   Anne, 15
Barker
   Joanna, 26, 42
   Thomas, 26, 42, 50
   Thomas Charles, 42
   William, 46, 58

Barker Jr
   William, 46
Barrallier
   Francis Louis, 10
Bathurst
   Henry, 63
Baxter
   James, 100
Beard
   Alfred Augustus Russell, 50
Bell
   Christian Leslie, 5
   Robin (Robert), 5
Bennett
   Alfred, 100
Bensley
   Henry, 48
Bent
   Ellis, 6, 33, 46, 71, 73
Bergin
   Edward, 6
Berry
   Mr and Mrs R., 53
Betts
   Harold Charles Henry, 25
Bibb
   John, 62
Biffin
   Cecil John, 71
   Jane, 37
   Louisa, 37
Birch
   Lieutenant John, 33
   Mary Arabella, 33
Blackman
   George Albert, 100
   John, 70
   Samuel, 21, 48
Blattman
   Michael, 49
   Owen Fendick, 68
Blaxcell
   Garnham, 24
Blaxland
   Dame Helen, 10
   Gregory, 20, 24

Index to Landowners, Tenants, and Others

John, 68
Bleeck
    Dr John, 48
Blow
    Catherine Ann, 68
Boardman
    Christine Loris, 4
    John, 24
    Noel Frederick, 4
    William, 28, 40
Bostock
    Robert, 27
Boulton
    John, 8
Bourke
    Thomas, 9
    William Joseph, 100
Bowring
    Paul and Margaret, 25
Brackfield
    John, 8
Bransby
    Dr George, 8
Brennan
    Thomas, 45, 53
Brennand
    Thomas, 45
Brent
    Herbert Kendall, 56
Bridgeman
    Alice, 22
Brooks
    Captain Richard, 25
Broughton
    Bishop, 61
    Mary Ann Broughton, 18
    William, 18
Bruchhauser
    Ernest John, 27
    Johann, 10
    Johann (John), 27
Buckle
    Francis, 65
Bugden
    Elizabeth, 100
    Henry, 100
Buggy
    Anne, 10
    Michael, 10, 73
Burcher
    Albert Stephen, 54
Burge
    Eric William, 70
Burgess
    Rev John Barry, 63
Burrell
    Emma Catherine, 4
Busby
    James, 45
Butler
    Gordon Hilder, 37
    James, 53
    Mabel Winifred (Poppy), 37
    Percival Ernest, 13
Byrnes
    John Henry (Don), 54

C

Caley
    George, 26, 58, 66
Camden
    Lord, 12, 13
Campbell
    Charles, 27
    David Malcolm, 53
    Dugald, 71
    Hugh, 21
    John Thomas, 4, 17, 37, 58
    Robert Bruce, 20
    William Douglas, 32, 34, 50
Carmagnola
    Francesco Giuseppe, 6
Carne
    Mary Ann, 18
    Thomas, 18
Carpenter
    Horatio, 18
Carroll
    Thomas, 13
Carter
    John, 100
Cavenagh
    Philip, 29
Chalker
    William, 19, 51, 67
    William Charles, 71
Champion
    Raymond George, 72
Channell
    William, 19
Channell Jr.
    William, 19
Chapplle
    Jane Briton, 42
Charker

Index to Landowners, Tenants, and Others

    William, 27, 110
Cheeke
    Alfred, 67
Chesham
    Bartley Horace, 10
    John, 19
    Lillian May, 19
Chester (horse), 39
Childs
    John William, 19, 100
Chisholm
    Dr Edwin, 100
    James, 10, 11, 22, 31, 39
    James Jr, 10
    James Sr, 31
Chittick
    Linda Muriel, 64
    Thomas, 56, 64
    Wilfred Thomas, 64
Chong
    Hop Chong, 35
Clark
    Patrick, 51
Clarke
    Captain William Henry, 20
    James, 100
Cleary
    Daniel James, 48
    William Daniel, 3
Cliff
    John W, 100
Clifton
    Cecil William, 65
    Henry Sivyer, 100
Clinch
    Clifford, 44
    Edith, 44
Clissold
    Charles, 42
Clout
    Charles, 56
    Edward Michael, 100
Coghill
    John, 38
Coker
    George, 42
Condell
    Ousley, 22
Condron
    John, 22, 64
Connor
    Owen, 22

Cooper
    George William, 8
Cordeaux
    William, 39
Coull
    William, 64
Cowper
    Rev William, 3, 70
    Sir Charles, 52, 70
    Thomas, 20
    William Charles, 41
Cox
    Phillip, 10
    Thomas, 8
Cox Jr
    William, 29
Cox Sr
    William, 29
Crace
    Edward John Lingen, 33, 43
Cranfield
    Catherine Ann, 68
    Clarence Herbert, 68
    Frederick Laurie, 55
    Thomas, 60
    William John, 16
Crawford
    Robert, 44
Crear
    James, 23
Creaser
    James, 23
Crerar
    James, 23
Crick
    William, 100
Croft
    Samuel, 24
Crookston
    Dr Robert Melville, 25
Cross
    Charles Norman, 36
Cross Jnr
    Ephraim, 10
Cross Jr
    Ephraim, 10
Crossing
    Percy, 41
Cubitt
    Daniel, 70
Cummings
    Benjamin, 24

Index to Landowners, Tenants, and Others

John, 24
Patrick, 24
Thomas, 53
Curran
   Michael, 24
Curry
   Daniel, 51
   James John, 8
Cuthel
   Mrs, 57

D

Damer
   Ashley Dawson, 50
Dangar
   Henry, 41
Daniels
   Annie Emily (Nan), 68
Davidson
   Walter Stevenson, 6
Davies
   Evan Alfred, 16, 47, 100
   Llewella Hope Evan, 16, 47
Davy
   Abraham, 34
Dawes
   William, 54
Dawson
   Kathleen Annie, 37
   Peter, 37
   Thomas, 9, 69, 99
   William Miller, 37
Dawson-Damer
   Hon Lionel John Seymour, 50
De Arrietta
   Jean Baptiste Lehimas, 45, 59
de Kerilleau
   Gabriel Louis Marie Huon, 10, 31, 36
De Kerilleau
   Gabriel Louis Marie Huon, 36
De Rosa
   John, 55
Dengate
   Edward Joseph, 50
   Elizabeth Mary, 45
   Frank, 11
   Frank Hercules, 33
   Frederick James, 11, 45
Dickson
   Joanna, 26, 42
   John, 25, 35, 42, 49, 50, 57
Donnelly

Russell Frank, 54
Donohue
   Jack, 7, 26
Douglass
   Arthur, 26
   Henry Grattan, 26
Doust
   Arthur Ebeneezer, 50
   Bertha Florist, 10
   Charles Ernest, 4
   David, 100
   Elizabeth Mary, 45
   Emma Catherine, 4
   Frederick Joseph, 10, 40, 58
Dowdall
   Michael, 26
Dowle
   Charles William, 100
Downes
   Frederick William Arthur, 9
   Katie May Elizabeth Coghill, 4
   Rupert Frederick Arding, 4
Downey
   Bridget, 53
Druitt
   Edward Frederick, 26
   Robert Henry, 25
Drummond
   John, 18, 27
Dunbar
   Arthur Hamilton Milton, 39
   John, 19
Dunk Jr
   Jesse, 28
Dunn
   Anna Marie Houghan, 66
   Charles Augustus, 66
   George Lambert, 60

E

Eagles
   Eric Essington, 52
Edmondson
   John Hurst, 27
   Joseph William, 27
Edrop
   James, 27
Edwards
   Rev Trevor, 63
Ellis
   Samuel, 28
Elphinstone

Index to Landowners, Tenants, and Others

J B, 62
Elyard
   William, 69
Emily
   Annie Emily (Nan), 68
English
   Herbert Thomas, 16

F

Fabert
   Mary, 47
Fairfax
   Warwick, 34, 50
Faithfull
   Frances Lillian, 3, 17
Faithfull-Anderson, 3, 17, 22, 51
Farrell
   Francis Andrew, 72
Farindon, 61
Fenning
   George, 100
Ferguson
   Francis, 29, 100
Fidkin
   Urban, 19
   William, 19
Field
   Barron, 36
   Barron, 36
   Julia, 9
Fletcher
   Constable Edward, 29
   Henrietta, 29
Forbes
   Mary Arabella, 33
Forrest
   Rev Robert, 61
Fowler
   Samuel, 50
Fox
   Philip John (Jack), 14
Franklin
   Jane, 37
   John Lunt, 37
   Louisa, 37
French
   Annie, 13, 24
Friend
   Walter, 45
Fryer
   Caroline, 36
   John, 100

Fryer:, 8
Fuller
   David and Lyndell, 71
   George, 100
Funnell
   James, 7
   Mary Ann Rebecca, 7
   Thomas, 100
Furner
   Charles, 25, 27, 44, 51, 65, 71
   Eliza Ann, 51
   Emma Margaret, 71
   Walter Charles, 100
Furner Jr.
   Charles, 27
Fyffe
   Edith, 44

G

Galvin
   Ada Harriet, 48
   John, 13
   Thomas, 30
Game
   Governor Phillip, 57
Gaunt
   John, 21
Goodluck
   Joseph Thomas, 13
Gordon
   Violet Marguerite, 5, 47
   William, 41
Gore
   William, 28
Gors
   Kathleen Annie, 37
Graham
   John, 32, 54
   John Joseph, 54
Gray
   Charles, 28, 70
   Edward, 5
   Joseph Charles, 70
Greentree
   Blanche, 37
Greenwood
   James, 31
Griffiths
   Edward George, 100
Grimes
   George, 33
Gurner

Index to Landowners, Tenants, and Others

John, 36

H

Hall
  Edward Smith, 20, 33
  Winifred, 16
Halvorsen
  Lars, 4
Hansen
  Lars Christian, 25
Harper
  George, 3, 30
Hassall
  James, 23, 24, 30
  Jonathan, 24, 42
  Rev Thomas, 23, 25, 34, 51, 53, 62, 63, 64, 67, 70
  Rowland, 23, 24, 26, 34, 41, 45, 64
  Samuel Otto, 8, 24
Havard
  Olive, 6
Havard
  Ward, 6
Hawkey
  Fanny Rundle, 35
  Richard, 66
  Richard Ernest, 11
Hayter
  Jeremiah, 32
Head
  H., 100
Heath
  Ben, 70
Hedley
  Gladys Ivy, 6
  James, 6
Hennessy
  Michael Laurence, 34
Herbert
  John Kelly, 35
  Thomas, 35
Herzog
  Anton Bernhard, 35
Hilder
  James, 51
Hindes, 61
Hoare
  Samuel, 26
Hoddle
  Surveyor Robert, 63
Hodge
  Maud, 6
  Philip Benjamin (Ben), 6

Hogg
  John Llewelyn, 39
Holz
  Jane Briton, 42
  William, 35, 38, 42
Hook
  Charles, 25
Hordern
  Anthony, 31, 70
Hore
  Norman Thomas, 56
Hosking
  John Edward, 36, 52, 58, 65
  William, 36, 52, 58
Hovell
  Captain William Hilton, 33, 47
Howe
  William, 28, 31, 45
Howey
  John Werge, 36
Hughes
  John Terry, 36, 40, 65
Hunt
  John Horbury, 17, 60
Hunter
  Governor John, 23, 46
  Matthew Dysart, 26, 42, 49, 50
Huntley
  William James, 100
Hurst
  Maude Elizabeth, 27
Hutchinson
  William, 9
Huthnance
  Albert Stevens, 22
  Alice, 22
  Maud, 6

I

Ibbetson
  Victor Edward, 53
Inglis
  Lorna Mary, 4
  Richard Reginald, 4
  Thomas, 23, 34, 43
  William, 15, 23

J

Jackson
  Dr William Hardy, 25, 100
  John, 32, 37
Jamison

Index to Landowners, Tenants, and Others

Sir John, 11, 23
Jarvis
  Jane, 37
Jefferis
  Dr James Tatham Whittell, 35
  Ethel Rachel Ward, 35
Jenkins
  Dr Richard Lewis, 48
Johnson
  John, 100
  Sarah Susan née Tavener, 100
Johnston
  Major George, 37
  Robert, 31, 37

K

Keaton
  Cornelius David, 53
Kelloway
  George William, 100
  John Thomas, 100
Kelly
  Thomas Hussey, 19
Kemp
  Charles, 8
Kendrick
  Atwill George, 50
Kenna
  Anne, 10
Kennerley
  Alfred, 37
Kenny
  Dr William, 38
Kidd
  John, 7
King
  Rev Cecil John, 38
Kitchen
  Henry, 27, 35
Knight
  Isaac, 26

L

Lakeman
  John, 8, 13, 71
Lambe
  Edward, 39
Lambert
  George Washington Thomas, 70
Larkin
  Willie, 12, 48, 56, 100
Lassetter
  Major Henry Beauchamp, 9
Lavercombe
  Clara Letitia Margaret, 46
  Edward, 46
Laycock
  Thomas, 37, 39
  Thomas William, 22
  William, 22, 31, 39
Le Fevre
  John, 39, 58
Linn
  Robert, 40
Longley
  Ellen Jean, 72
  Jack, 72
Loomes
  John Edward, 40
  William, 40
Lord
  Edward, 50
Lowe
  Barbara, 9
  Edwin Frederick, 28
  Robert, 7, 9, 49
Lucas
  Penelope, 40

M

Macarthur
  Elizabeth, 5, 13, 14, 21, 22, 40, 41, 60
  Hannibal Hawkins, 26, 28, 34, 69
  James, 6, 12, 57, 59, 61
  John, 9, 10, 12, 13, 18, 19, 34, 35, 40, 49, 59, 66, 69
  William, 6, 12, 29, 30, 43, 59, 61
Macarthur-Onslow
  Arthur John (Jack), 5, 47
  Christian Leslie, 5
  Edward Arthur, 16
  Elizabeth, 13, 14, 21, 41, 60
  Francis Arthur, 41
  Lt. Col. (later Brigadier General) George MacLeay, 5, 47
  Lt. Col. (later Major General) James William, 30
  Major General Sir Denzil, 45
Macarthur-Onslow
  Violet Marguerite, 5
Macarthur-Onslow
  Violet Marguerite, 47
Macaulay
  William, 4
MacLeay

Index to Landowners, Tenants, and Others

Alexander, 9, 31
George, 5, 9, 47
Macpherson
   Allan, 6
   William, 6
Macquarie
   Governor Lachlan, 5, 37, 39, 51, 58
Maddrell
   Katie May Elizabeth Coghill, 4
Maher
   John, 101
Malcolm
   George Norman, 72
Maloney
   Daniel Francis, 19
Mann
   Ashley Dawson, 50
Mansfield
   George Allen, 62
Marden
   John, 40
Marr
   Henry Edward, 36, 42
Marsden
   Rev Samuel, 63
   Reverend Samuel, 34
Marshall
   R, 101
Martin
   Commander Alexander, 17
   John Benson, 3
Mason
   Thomas Henry, 21
Maxwell
   Gerald Verner, 41
May
   Percy Withers, 101
McAlister
   Lachlan, 40
   Matthew, 41
McBeth
   J, 60
McCallum
   Emma Margaret, 71
McCaughney
   Minnie Arthur, 25
McCullan
   Theresa, 31
McCulloch
   Alexander, 39, 101
McDonagh
   James Henry, 35
McDonald

   George Frederick, 32
   James, 37
   Miss Lorna, 37
McEvoy, 37
McEwan
   Elaine Dawn, 37
McInnes
   Vaughan and Sue, 27
McIntosh
   brothers, 71
   Charles Stewart McIntosh, 25
   Lorna Mary, 4
   Ronald Andrew, 5
McKinnon
   Donald, 45
McKnight
   Andrew, 30
McLean
   Christine Loris, 4
   Sarah, 4
McMahon
   Mr, 64
McMinn
   John Thomas, 8, 30
McNiven
   Malcom, 4
   Sarah, 4
Meehan
   James, 20
Middlehurst
   Sarah, 12, 41
Milford
   John, 12
   Sarah, 12, 41
   Sarah Middlehurst née, 12
Miller
   James Lovell, 101
   Peter, 5
Mitchell
   David Edward, 54
   Elizabeth Broughton Huon, 36
   Sir Thomas Livingstone, 29
   Thomas, 12
   Thomas Livingstone, 29, 48
   William, 36
Moffitt
   Gordon, 30
Molle
   George James, 18, 45, 48
   Lieutenant Governor George James, 45, 48
Moore
   Arthur Barrington, 54
   Caroline, 54

    Edward, 28, 31, 34, 64
    Edward Lomas, 4, 50
    Henry (dec'd), 101
    James Gray, 31
    John Edward, 28, 64, 101
    Joseph, 31
    Robert Besting, 29, 31
    Thomas, 45
    William, 54
Moran
    Family, 65
Murdoch
    Peter, 9, 31
Myles
    Charles, 58
    James Alexander, 58

N

Napper
    Robert William, 68
Nepean
    Evan, 48
Nesbitt
    Richard Johnson, 48
Nettleton
    Joseph, 48
New
    Charles Edward, 101
    Mary Ann Rebecca, 7
Nixon
    Frederick, 47
Northan
    Charles, 65

O

O'Connor
    Ethel Kate, 46
Onslow
    Arthur Foot, 19, 29
    Captain Arthur Alexander Walton, 29, 50
Ousley
    Major Gen. Sir Ralph Ousley, 22
Owen
    Winifred, 16
Oxley
    John, 51
    John Joseph William Molesworth, 17, 27, 38, 51
    John Norton, 38

P

Packenham
    William, 48
Page
    Bridget, 53
    Charles, 21, 53, 59
Pain
    Rev Arthur Wellesley, 62, 63
Paling
    William Henry, 18, 32, 101
Palmer
    George Thomas, 52
Parrott
    William, 52, 64
Payne
    William Charles, 64
Pear
    Matthew, 52
Peat
    Arthur Melville (Mel), 23
    John, 4, 17, 19, 30, 35, 65, 67, 68, 71, 101
Pepper
    Maria Louise, 67
Perkins
    Thomas Emanuel, 67
Perry
    John Theodore, 50
Peters
    Walter Frederick, 35, 101
Phillip
    Governor Arthur, 48
Picken
    Robert John, 25
Picton
    Sir Thomas Picton, 53
Pinkerton
    James Frederick John, 14, 101
Piper
    Captain John, 5, 27
Poole
    Alfred Cecil, 68
    Frank Elias George, 101
    John William, 101
Porter
    George Alexander, 22, 43, 101
Pritchard
    William, 41
Pulling
    Joseph, 35
Purcell
    John, 37
Pye
    Colonel John Bruce, 20, 33

Index to Landowners, Tenants, and Others

Q

Quinlan
    Ethel Rachel Ward, 35

R

Rae
    Stanley Seaton, 69
    Thomas Howard Elwin, 69
Rapley
    Eliza Jane, 101
    Frederick George, 58
    Thomas, 44
Rawlinson
    Robert, 68
Ray
    Elaine Dawn, 37
    Milton Brettell, 37
Raymond
    James, 66
Reed
    Isaac Reed, 55
Reeve
    Thora Haroldene (Peg), 53
Reeves
    Henry Pollock, 55, 61, 101
Reid
    Charles, 22
    Isaac, 55
Rheinberger
    Peter Joseph, 56
Richardson
    Mabel Winifred (Poppy), 37
    Mary, 47
Riley
    Alexander, 54
Ritchie
    William Cochrane, 56
Roach
    John, 55
Roberts
    John, 44
    Thomas, 28
Robertson
    Larry and Mickey, 32
Rofe
    John Stewart, 37, 50
    William, 60
Rogers
    Rev Edward, 27, 62
Rootes
    James, 101
Rose
    Thomas, 45
Ross
    Daniel MacLaine, 58
Royer
    Ernest Louis Henry, 29
Ruard
    Cyril, 16
Rudd
    Thomas, 34, 42
Rümker
    Charles Ludwig Christian, 63
Russell
    Captain William, 58
    William, 58
Rutter
    William James, 21, 71

S

Salter
    James Albert, 101
Sandrone
    Joseph, 39
Sarina
    Gordon Howard Conrad, 64
Scott
    Sir Walter, 3
Scriven
    Henrietta, 29
Shadforth
    Henry Tudor, 55
    Lieutenant Colonel Thomas, 55
Sharman
    James, 58
Sharpe
    George, 58
    Mary, 5
Sheather
    James, 58, 101
Sheil
    Thomas, 11
Shelley
    William James, 58
Sheppard
    Mabel, 33
Ship
    Timothy, 52
Sibraa
    Patrick Philip, 71
Sidman
    Alice Gertrude, 17
    George Victor, 17
    William, 7

Simpson
    Alexander, 21
    Ebeneezer, 21, 53, 59, 71, 101
    Ebeneezer Jr, 101
Simpson Jr
    Ebeneezer, 59
Simpson Sr
    Ebeneezer, 59
Sloan
    Peter, 101
Small
    Fredrick Leslie, 21
    James, 42
    Mary Ann Small, 42
Smart
    Charles Thomas, 25
    Charles Wesley, 43
    Leslie Charles William (Les), 59
Smith
    Archbishop William Samaurez, 62
    Charles Philip, 101
    Henry, 56
    Jane, 56
    Thomas, 60, 101
    Walter Thomas, 60
    William, 101
Smythe
    Richard, 8
Southwell
    Howard Carlyle, 7, 48
    John Carlyle, 6
Spear
    Eric William Sutherland, 42
Speed
    John, 59
Spice
    Henry, 101
Stevens
    Bob, 10
Stimson
    Eliza Ann, 51
    William, 101
Stratford
    Mary, 5
Stuckey
    Alan, 67
    Nurse E Jean, 6
    Walter, 101
Sturt
    Captain Charles, 9
    Charles, 9, 66
Sullivan
    Jeremiah, 27
Sulman, 5, 13, 14, 30, 60
    Sir John, 13, 14
Sutton
    Sir Frederick, 38
Swan
    Arthur, 34

T

Taber
    George, 36, 43
Taber Jr
    Thomas, 43
Taber Sr
    Thomas, 43
Taplin
    Alfred Edwin, 57, 101
    Frederick William, 57
    William John, 101
    William Leslie, 8
Tavener
    Sarah Susan, 100
Tegel
    Albert Arthur (Bert), 53
    Max, 71
    Thora Haroldene (Peg), 53
Tench
    Captain Watkin, 54
Testoni
    Feruccio (Frederick) Lino, 31
    Theresa, 31
Therry
    Father, 30
Thomas
    Ellen Jean, 72
    Henry Arding, 70
Thompson
    Anne, 15
    Charles Augustus, 12, 101
    Henry, 9, 12, 15, 16, 41, 65
    Joseph, 52
    Samuel Herbert, 15
Thomson
    Annette Lillie, 42
    Elizabeth Gillies, 42
    Ninian Alan, 42
Thorn
    Charles, 101
    Joyce, 21
    Keith, 21
    Norman, 30
Throsby

Index to Landowners, Tenants, and Others

    Charles, 59
Thurn
    Martin, 42
    Philip, 66
Tickner
    Edward, 11
    John, 45
Tiffin
    Sarah, 12, 41
Tingcombe
    Rev Henry, 61
Townson
    Robert, 66
Tritton
    Alfred John, 101
Tucker
    Rita, 71
    Rupert, 48, 71
Tulloh
    Archibald (Archie), 4

V

Verge
    John, 14, 62
Vicary
    Albert Edward, 21, 67
    Caroline, 36
    Ida Elsie Mary, 36
    James Robert, 36
Victoria
    Mabel, 33
von Frankenberg
    Baron Frederick Elliott, 60
Vyse
    Charles, 19

W

Wales
    George Henry, 7
Waley
    Frederick, 46
Walker
    Dr Josiah Wesley Walker, 3
    Eliza Cordelia, 26
    Rowland Thomas Brisbane, 26
Wallace
    William, 70
Walley
    Ethel Kate, 46
Walsh
    Eustace Henry, 101
Warby
    John, 32
Ward
    Paddy, 51
Warrand
    James Lingen, 30
Wasson
    James, 101
Waters
    Charles, 24, 67
Waterworth
    James Edwin, 24
Watson
    Robert, 56
Watt
    Captain Oswald, 70
Watts
    Hugh Gritton, 39
    Margaret Clara, 39
Weaver
    William, 12
Wentworth
    George, 33, 46
    John, 43
    William Charles, 67
West
    Dr Francis William, 41
    Mary, 23
    Obed, 67
    Thomas, 67
Whatmore
    George Willoughby, 30
Wheatley
    Leslie William Roy, 70
    William Alfred, 53
Wheeler
    Bertha Florist, 10
    Edmund, 101
    James, 102
    Raymond Charles, 10
    Walter, 65
White
    Reuben, 20
    Robert, 9
    The Hon. James, 16, 17, 38, 39, 41
Whiteman, 72
    Alice Gertrude, 17
    Charles Thomas, 102
    Francis, 72
    Frederick Keith, 43, 56
    James Butchers, 49
    Keith, 23
    Marjory, 23
    Mr F C, 61

Index to Landowners, Tenants, and Others

Nelson Thomas, 59
Whittington
    Alfred Bernard, 22
Whybrow
    Edward, 9
    Julia, 9
    William, 48
    William Edward, 9
Whyte
    Florence June, 12
    Leo Daniel, 12
Wignell
    William Walter, 69
Wild
    John Benton, 70
    John Henry, 35, 50, 64, 66
Wilkinson
    Rev Frederick, 35
    William, 102
Willard
    Barbara, 9
Williams
    John, 35
    Ray, 27
Willis
    Timothy, 33
Wills
    James (Jim), 39
Wood
    Sarah, 30
Woodhill
    Frank Leslie, 67
    Maria Louise, 67
Woodhouse
    Edmund Hume, 45
Worgan
    Surgeon George Bouchier, 54, 71
Wright
    Blanche, 37
    Charles Henry David, 37
    Guy Francis, 3
Wylie
    Gerlad Douglas, 25
    Minnie Arthur, 25

Y

Yewen
    Elizabeth, 72
    John, 72

www.ingramcontent.com/pod-product-compliance
Lightning Source LLC
Chambersburg PA
CBHW041711290426
44109CB00028B/2843